AGAINST PUBLIC BROADCASTING

WHY WE SHOULD PRIVATISE THE ABC AND HOW TO DO IT

Chris Berg and Sinclair Davidson

AGAINST PUBLIC BROADCASTING

WHY WE SHOULD PRIVATISE THE ABC AND HOW TO DO IT

Chris Berg and Sinclair Davidson

Connor Court Publishing 2018

First published in 2018 by Connor Court Publishing Pty Ltd

ISBN: 9781925501896

Connor Court Publishing Pty Ltd
Suite 2, 146 Boundary Street
West End, Queensland, Australia, 4101

sales@connorcourt.com
www.connorcourtpublishing.com.au
Phone 0497 900 685

Contents

1 Introduction

The Australian Broadcasting Corporation is a $1.04 billion public policy program. This book treats it as exactly that: a government intervention into the market for news, entertainment and communications. Policy interventions are costly. The ABC represents a billion dollars taken out of taxpayers' pockets and not used on other government priorities. Policy interventions are also costly in a non-monetary sense. They can have unintended or counterproductive consequences. They can crowd out non-government activity, stifle entrepreneurship or technological innovation, distort the marketplace, systemically favour particular political interests and ideologies, and create fiefdoms of unaccountable bureaucrats.

We argue in this book that the ABC is an anachronism. It was established in a moment of history significantly unlike our own, facing a cultural and political environment greatly different to our own, with technological and economic challenges completely opposite to those we now face. Over the course of eight decades the ABC has embedded itself in the Australian political system and public consciousness. But the original rationales for the ABC have expired. Australia's politics and culture have changed. Technology has made the concerns of Australian policy makers in the 1930s—or even the 1990s, when the ABC was last subjected to a major review—redundant or anachronistic. Economic justifications for a state-owned media broadcaster simply do not fit the modern media landscape.

The arguments for public broadcasting in the twenty-first century are simply not compelling. It is certainly the case that the ABC has bound within it an enormous amount of cultural capital as a consequence of its eighty years of pre-eminence in the Australian media industry. But that should not be confused with either a claim that a publicly-funded broadcaster was necessary to build that cultural capital or that Australian culture would suffer in a world where the ABC had been reformed or privatised.

The ABC is an Australian 'icon' in the same sense that the Commonwealth Bank was an icon before its privatisation, and in the same anachronistic sense that Qantas (as the 'national carrier') is imagined by some to be an essential part of the Australian psyche. We can celebrate the achievements of the ABC, its cultural significance, and its role in Australian history. But that should not prevent us from looking sceptically at whether the ABC remains good public policy—as we should with all costly government interventions into the economy and society. Does the ABC have a good reason to exist, now? Are the benefits of public broadcasting worth the cost? What could the ABC do differently, or better, or not at all?

When the ABC was established in 1932, the Australian media landscape consisted of a handful of newspapers in each city and country town, magazines, newsreels shown at the local cinema, and the nascent radio industry. The first experimental broadcast in Australia occurred in 1919. Broadcasting only officially began in 1923. Twelve years later there were just 350,000 paid radio listeners across the Australian continent—less than five per cent of the population.[1] The entry price to join this new technology was steep: a basic three-valve radio receiver sold for at least $1,600 in 2016 dollars. A more prestigious model would cost upwards of $3,500.[2] Receivers sold in 1938 declared that they were large enough to be operated standing up: 'No squat, no stoop, no squint'.[3] Broadcasters urged listeners to 'stay at home and be entertained'.[4] In the first years of the Great Depression, broadcasting was an infant technology, and the idea of the broadcast media as a distinct ecosystem and influence on Australian politics and culture was a topic of great speculation. The Country Party leader Earle Page pronounced that it 'shares with aviation the distinction of being the most wonderful achievement of humanity of the last quarter of a century … capable of rendering incalculable service to mankind, for it has annihilated distance, space and time'.[5] The technology was new enough for Wireless Weekly to declare on the eve of the 1932 election that 'It's a Wireless Election'.[6]

Eighty years has seen a complete revolution in the amount of media available to Australian consumers, the types of media available, and the content of that media. Today, listening to radio ranks just below reading newspapers as a top-three preferred entertainment activity with 17 per cent and 19 per cent of Australians respectively. By contrast, watching television is rated as a top-three preferred entertainment activity by 62 per cent of Australians, followed closely by using the internet for social or personal interests at 60 per cent.[7] Radio is as likely to be delivered digitally over the internet, with dozens of digital radio channels in Australia alone, or online through radio station archives.

Permanent, universal internet access means that the 84 per cent of Australians who own a modern smartphone have instant access to hundreds of thousands of radio stations streaming around the world, and hundreds of thousands more podcasts.[8] Apple estimated that there were 250,000 unique podcasts in 2013—a number which will certainly have multiplied in recent years as this format has embedded itself deeper into popular culture. Other radio-like services like Spotify and Apple Music deliver algorithmically personalised music playlists, making the number of radio 'stations' effectively infinite.

Through ubiquitous high-speed internet connections at home and on the 4G phone networks that blanket the continent, Australians enjoy instantaneous access to virtually anything the global media supplies. In the evening they 'binge' watch programs on streaming services like Netflix and Stan. Netflix is an American company which began in 1997 as a mail order company for DVDs, but now is its own production and distribution network, releasing some of this decade's most culturally significant programming in nearly 200 countries. Netflix's first Australian production, the supernatural crime drama *Tidelands*, was announced in 2017.

Audiences expect to be able to personally engage with what they are reading, watching or listening to, either through comments sections at the bottom of articles or on social media. More than 15 million Australians are on Facebook, and more than five million are on Twitter.[9] They are more likely to discover new content to watch, read and listen to, and new products to buy, through recommendations on social media than through advertising on television, radio or print.[10]

If anything, this snapshot understates the revolutionary changes that have occurred in the media over the last eighty-five years. It is sometimes hard for us to replicate the mindset of even one or two generations earlier, particularly when it comes to something as prosaic as media consumption. Humans quickly acclimatise to changes in technology. For the radio listeners of the 1930s—themselves a tiny minority of Australia's population—once something had been missed on the radio it was gone forever. Technical problems often ruined radio performances that may have been in preparation for weeks.[11] Indeed, this was the experience of media consumption until home taping and the VCR were introduced in the 1970s and 1980s. If you were not at home for a favourite radio or television show, you would not expect to hear or see it again.

Today, we expect our news and entertainment to be available on demand, in a format of our choosing, on a device of our choosing, and to be able to pause and resume that news and entertainment at will. Just the invention of the VCR was revolutionary. Home videos encouraged the 'audience to become nomadic, upsetting the billion-dollar industry devoted to pinning it down', writes the media scholar Frederick Wasser.[12] We are now a long way past the idea that the audience can be 'pinned down'; a long way past the idea that we are dependent on the gatekeepers of print, radio and television to direct our attention as they see fit. The 'media' is no longer a set of distinct, programmed, curated and scheduled distribution platforms. It is an endlessly diverse, endlessly individualised network, entirely at the control of the user.

What role does public broadcasting have in this radically changed environment? At the very least, the dramatic changes in technology and media over the last few decades should have led to a deep rethink of the purpose of public broadcasting—and whether it is still necessary in this new era. Yet such a rethink has not seriously occurred. The ABC has used all the new technology to expand its products and experiment with new approaches. The ABC's Charter gives it nearly unlimited capacity to choose what it delivers, limited only by the appropriations it receives from the federal government. It is no surprise that it has sought to expand as the cost of broadcasting through the internet has virtually dropped to zero. The ABC is a bureaucracy, after all, and like all bureaucracies it wants to grow its influence, prominence, prestige and budget. But this does not mean an expanding and entrepreneurial ABC is in the interests of media consumers, the media industry or taxpayers.

Public broadcasting arose in response to specific institutional, economic and technological needs. Our needs are much different—the polar opposite of what they were in 1932, or even 1983, when the ABC was corporatised.

The control of broadcasting

The ABC has been the subject of a number of excellent histories—most notably Ken Inglis' two volume *This is the ABC* and *Whose ABC?*, and Alan Thomas' *Broadcast and be*

Damned.[13] But it has been subject to surprisingly little serious analysis as a policy initiative since it was established. The questions which we usually pose when scrutinising government policies are rarely posed to the ABC. Is it cost effective? Does it achieve the goals which it has been set? Are those goals still relevant? Are there better, cheaper, less costly ways to achieve those goals? We press these questions on almost every public policy initiative except the ABC.

Only a few times in its history has the existence and purpose of the ABC been subject to this sort of top-down scrutiny. The legislation for the ABC was pushed through in a period of high economic and political drama—at the height of the Great Depression in Australia and in the wake of the Labor split of 1931. A royal commission into wireless broadcasting just a few years earlier had conspicuously not recommended the establishment of a public broadcaster.[14] When a parliamentary committee inquiry in 1942 investigated the wireless industry, it offered few clues as to what the government had in mind as a goal for public broadcasting.[15]

Subsequent reviews have either avoided reckoning with the policy purpose of public broadcasting, or given the question a brief and unsatisfactory treatment. The first major review into the ABC was commissioned by the Fraser government, just under fifty years since it was established. The Committee of Review of the Australian Broadcasting Commission, known colloquially as the 'Dix Review' for its chair Alex Dix, affirmed the continued existence of the public broadcaster but laid the foundation for its restructure as a corporation.[16] One of the early legislative programs of the Hawke government in 1983 was to bring about this change, inaugurating the Australian Broadcasting Corporation. A departmental review five years later proposed dividing ABC operations into Charter and non-Charter operations, but nothing came of this proposal.[17]

The next major review into the ABC occurred under the Howard government. The Mansfield Review, commissioned immediately after the 1996 election, recommended that the ABC Charter provide tighter direction, and that the ABC should rely more on outsourcing, but its engagement with the purpose of public broadcasting was minimal.[18] The Howard government commissioned a further review by the consulting firm KPMG to identify inefficiencies in the ABC in 2006, and the Abbott government conducted an efficiency study in 2014, but neither of these resulted in a serious consideration of the purposes of public broadcasting.[19]

In his 1988 book *Breaking Up the ABC*, the public policy scholar (and subsequently vice-chancellor of the University of Melbourne) Glyn Davis characterised the ABC as a confused organisation, struggling with the contradictions of its Charter, the ambiguities about the purpose of public broadcasting, its relationship to commercial broadcasting, the parliament's desire that the broadcaster prioritise both national and regional markets, and tensions over whether to target elite tastes or popular tastes. As a consequence 'the ABC has vacillated', Davis wrote, 'sometimes playing to its small but loyal and politically influential audience, sometimes reaching for a wider, national public'.[20] Davis concluded that the ABC should be rationalised, its purpose clarified, and many of its programs sold off, tendered out and deconstructed. Yet Davis rejected privatisation, arguing that to sell the ABC would 'trade illusory financial security for purpose'.[21] Much hinges on what we think that purpose is.

This book seeks to tackle what we think is the main policy question head on: why should we have a public broadcaster? In the early years of wireless broadcasting, nations had to make choices about how broadcasting should be controlled. The framework of new comparative economics, first developed by the Harvard economist Andrei Shleifer and various co-authors, conceptualises the choices of social control as a spectrum from market order to state control.[22] At one extreme, a country may rely on the discipline of the competitive marketplace to 'control' the media—punish bad behaviour through reputation and lost consumers. At the other extreme, the state could directly own the media. In between these two choices are a host of middling alternatives. Citizens may control the media by private litigation on ethical or property violations. Or the government could choose to impose regulation to control, but not directly own, the media.

Each of these strategies have costs, conceptualised as dictatorship costs (the costs imposed by the state) and disorder costs (the costs of a free market). Some industries and policy questions are more suited to one type of social control than another. For example, the disorder costs of market controlled policing are high enough that the potential dictatorship costs of state policing are tolerable. On the other hand, the disorder costs of a market in bread are not high enough to justify the dictatorship costs of state-run bakeries. Formally, our argument is that technological change has significantly lowered the disorder costs of relying on market discipline for the control of broadcasting. To the extent that state ownership of broadcasting was justifiable in the 1930s—and we are sceptical that it was—it certainly is no longer justifiable in the 2010s.

Globally, many governments own broadcasters and newspapers. In a 2003 paper published in the *Journal of Law and Economics*, Shleifer and three co-authors from the World Bank surveyed the patterns of media ownership in 97 countries around the world, including Australia. The question they investigated was: What explained the prevalence of state media ownership? If state media ownership was done primarily in the public interest—that is, introduced in order to resolve a social or economic problem caused by private media ownership—they hypothesised that it would be most common in countries which could keep dictatorship costs to a minimum. Public broadcasting would be a feature of free and liberal states whose governments were relatively benevolent and focused on their citizens' needs. Alternatively, if state ownership serviced the needs more of rulers and political elites, it would be most common in countries with weak and illiberal governments.

Shleifer and his co-authors concluded that public broadcasting was far more common in 'countries that are poorer, more autocratic, with lower levels of primary school enrollment, and with higher levels of state intervention in the economy'. Furthermore, 'countries with greater state ownership of the media have less free press, fewer political rights for citizens, inferior governance, less developed capital markets, and inferior health outcomes'.[23] While this does not prove that public broadcasting is a tool for state power in a developed, wealthy and stable democracy like Australia, it is a significant blow for the argument that public broadcasting is a necessary, rational response to clearly identified problems in media markets.

What is the ABC?

The ABC is a statutory authority, meaning it is a body established to implement the Australian Broadcasting Corporation Act 1983. That Act contains the ABC Charter (reproduced in the Appendix to this book). The Charter requires the ABC to produce 'innovative and comprehensive broadcasting services' that 'contribute to a sense of national identity', 'inform and entertain' and 'reflect the cultural diversity of the Australian community' within Australia. Outside Australia, the ABC is to transmit broadcasting programs that inform the world about Australia and Australian 'attitudes', and keep Australians overseas informed about Australian affairs. In this way, the Charter is an elaboration of the first statement of purpose provided in the 1932 Act:

> The Commission shall provide and shall broadcast from the national broadcasting stations adequate and comprehensive programmes and shall take in the interests of the community all such measures as, in the opinion of the Commission, are conducive to the full development of suitable broadcasting programmes.[24]

While the modern Charter is more specific than the directions contained in the 1932 Act, it is not significantly more specific. As a result, the ABC has extremely wide discretion about how to fulfil its obligations.

Two other parts of the modern Charter are worth noting. First, the Charter requires the ABC to 'encourage and promote the musical, dramatic and other performing arts in Australia', which reflects many of the original purposes and interests of the parliamentarians who established the ABC in the 1930s. Second, the Charter specifically notes that the ABC is 'to provide digital media services'. This was added to the Charter in 2013 by the then-Labor government; not to give the ABC new direction but to endorse what the ABC was already doing. The Hawke government's 1983 corporatisation was intended to give the ABC an entrepreneurial mindset, and by amending the Charter in 2013 the government was only playing catch-up. But as this apparently unobjectionable episode emphasises, what the Charter says and what the ABC does are not the same thing.

The Charter is at best only a loose guide to what the ABC does. Nor is it any constraint on ABC operations. While the Charter is spelled out in legislation, section 6(4) of the Charter explicitly states that 'Nothing in this section shall be taken to impose on the Corporation a duty that is enforceable by proceedings in a court.' Additionally, there is nothing in the Charter that could be described as an enforcement mechanism, nor are there any penalties detailed for potential breaches of the Charter.[25] The Charter is in law—insofar as it exists on the statute books—but it is not law.

The ABC is governed by a managing director that appoints to the ABC board. Under changes made to this process by the Rudd government, appointments to the ABC board are in turn nominated by a nomination panel, who provide the government of the day with recommended appointees. The ABC's 4,769 employees (4,093 full-time equivalent in 2017) are not, technically, public servants, as they are not employed under the Australian Public Service Act. But this is a legislative nicety, and of little analytical significance. The ABC derives 90 per cent of its revenue from annual government appropriations in order to pursue public service broadcasting: this makes ABC employees 'public servants' in every real sense.

The ABC is by any standard a major media conglomerate.[26] It runs four national radio networks—Radio National, the youth service Triple J, Classic FM, and ABC NewsRadio—eight capital city radio stations, and declares that it 'has a presence' in 48 regional locations. On digital radio it also offers Double J (a station for 'over 30s'), ABC Jazz, ABC Country, ABC Grandstand, Triple J Unearthed, and ABC Extra for special events. It runs four television channels: the main ABC channel, ABC2 (which runs children's content and young adult content), ABC3 (which runs exclusively children's content), and the round-the-clock news service ABC News 24. Its international network, Australia Plus, fulfils the Charter's requirement that it broadcast internationally. Online it offers a digital news service, producing online exclusive journalism, as well as a video-on-demand service, iView, with content drawn from its television networks but also produced exclusive to the service.

The ABC also has a substantial commercial arm. It has a network of more than 200 shops and outlets around the country. It produces and distributes DVDs and digital content. It resells its production facilities and assets for production in Australia, and resells digital, audio and photographic content. It publishes books and magazines and sells merchandise. Finally, it puts on and supports concerts and other live events. In 2015-16, for example, it put on a touring roadshow for *Play School* and the *Good Game Live,* and partnered with comedians and Opera Australia.

This potpourri of businesses and products is not unusual for a large media outlet. The ABC has experimented with a large range of products. One such experiment was 'ABC Island' in the 3D virtual environment *Second Life.* When this virtual ABC property was closed in 2012, it became an emblem of the ABC's susceptibility to fall for technological fads. Nevertheless, most media companies have a large range of interests and assets, and most seek to extract as much value out of their business as possible. All else being equal, firms should experiment. They should seek to bring new products to market. They should be entrepreneurial. But the ABC is not like other media companies. It is funded by taxation, which gives it privilege and power in the market which other firms do not enjoy. It is a policy initiative that needs limits, accountability, and a rule to 'do no harm' to the industry it dominates. Even if its policy rationale is woolly and aspirational—to 'contribute to a sense of the national identity'– the way it goes about that purpose needs to be grounded and utilitarian.

In the next chapter we provide a policy history of the origins of the ABC, and trace how its rationale for existence has developed and expanded over the last century. To understand the anachronism of the ABC it is necessary to understand where it came from: the world in which it was established, the problems it evolved to tackle, and the cultural and technological distance between then and now.

In Chapter 3 we then use that history to outline and critique the arguments for public broadcasting in the twenty-first century. We identify eight distinct arguments for public broadcasting that have been variously used to defend the ABC existence, and find them wanting. Some of these arguments have been made redundant by technological or social change. Others could be achieved more effectively and cheaply by targeted policy—subsidies or regulation, for instance—that did not require the Australian government to own and run a major media conglomerate.

Chapter 4 details costs and consequences of the ABC. We explore how viewing the ABC through three lenses—that of a bureaucracy, that of a non-profit firm, and that of a political actor—provides clarification about the burden of the ABC on the economic and political system, and how the broadcaster's behaviour can be explained. Too many critiques of the ABC are little more than a list of individual, specific complaints. Our goal in this chapter is not to itemise, but explain: for instance, if the ABC is biased towards one side of politics, then what institutional and organisational features have led to that?

In Chapter 5 we outline the options for reforming and privatising the ABC. We conclude that not only should the ABC be privatised, but it should be privatised in a way that its new owners have the most incentive to make it an ongoing success. Finally, in conclusion we outline what the world would look like without public broadcasting.

2 The origins of public broadcasting

The Australian broadcast industry is a hybrid of two systems: the American and the British. The American system is an almost completely private system, and the British system—at least in its original form—an almost completely state owned one.[1] Where the American radio industry was in its early days characterised by a profusion of stations, each supported by advertising and sponsorship, and a limited amount of regulatory control (beyond that imposed by spectrum management), British radio was provided by a monopoly, the British Broadcasting Corporation—financed by the licence fees paid by subscribers, without advertising, and heavily controlled. The Australian approach consisted of a publicly funded broadcaster competing with private, advertising-supported radio broadcasting. When television was introduced to Australia this structure was replicated for the new technology and the new commercial television broadcasters competed with the new ABC television service.

This hybrid system has left a deep mark on the structure and assumed purpose of public broadcasting in Australia. The ABC has always been unsure of its role: is it to provide what the commercial broadcasters do not, or to compete with commercial broadcasters on their own terms? Ambiguity in the ABC's mission has dogged the public broadcaster since its establishment. The Commonwealth parliament put little thought into defining the purpose of public broadcasting. Far from the result of a careful consideration about the need for public broadcasting and its relationship to the private broadcasters, the ABC came out of an environment of technological and regulatory confusion—the structural uncertainty and policy failures of the radio market in the 1920s.

Wireless before the ABC

Wireless communication in Australia dates back to 1888. Richard Threlfall, a practical-minded professor of physics at the University of Sydney (he had lost fingers while experimenting with explosives) had experimented with wireless just a year after Heinrich Hertz demonstrated control of electromagnetic waves in Germany.[2] In a paper presented in 1890, Threlfall proposed using wireless as a beacon to communicate: 'signaling, for instance, might be accomplished secretly by means of a sort of electric ray flasher, the signals being invisible to anyone not provided with a properly turned tube'.[3]

The fathers of Australian federation were well aware of the potential of this new technology. In the new Australian Constitution, the Commonwealth took responsibility for postal services, telegraphy and telephony. Threlfall's brother-in-law was the federation father Bernard Wise, who had also been a member of the Association for the Advancement of Science where Threlfall presented his 1890 paper. At the 1897-98 Constitutional Convention, Wise added the crucial phrase 'and like services' to the Constitution, giving the Commonwealth power over wireless—whatever that might end up being.[4]

Yet after this early interest, there was little activity on wireless during the first decade of the twentieth century. The introduction of wireless communication in Australia was slowed considerably by two factors: first was the political and economic power of the existing telegraphy and postal interests who saw the coming of wireless as a threat to their business models. The second was a rivalry between the British Post Office and the Marconi Company, which held the British patent for the most popular wireless technology.[5]

While the constitution gave the Commonwealth responsibility for wireless communication, specific legislative control over that technology still had to be established. In August 1905 the second Deakin government passed the Wireless Telegraphy Act. The legislation effectively nationalised the electromagnetic spectrum, which until then had effectively been a commons on which a few hobbyists and scientists could experiment. The act created 'a Government monopoly of wireless telegraphy in the Commonwealth', in the words of the Tasmanian senator John Keating, who introduced the bill.[6] From then on, users of the spectrum required a licence from the Postmaster-General's Department (PMG). The legislation was not controversial. As Ross Curnow writes, 'neither the desirability of nor the necessity for Government control over wireless telegraphy was questioned'.[7] Curnow suggests a further motive for the Commonwealth takeover: to prevent the Marconi Company from gaining an economic foothold in an uncontrolled environment. (The British government had passed similar legislation just one year earlier.)

Unsurprisingly, nationalising the radio spectrum did little to spur the rollout of wireless telegraphy. The establishment of a domestic competitor to the Marconi Company—Australasian Wireless Limited, using the German Telefunken technology—gave some hope to breaking the political impasse, but was quickly bogged down in litigation about the Marconi patent rights.[8] The Fisher Labor government established a second domestic firm, the Maritime Wireless Telegraph Company, this time under direct government control, using a new technology developed by a young Australian who had worked on telegraphy in England and Tsarist Russia. Maritime Wireless was also immediately bogged down in patent litigation, as both Marconi and Australasian Wireless used their weight against the new competitor. Marconi and Australasian Wireless merged on the eve of World War One, creating the Amalgamated Wireless Company of Australasia (AWA), just in time for control of the spectrum to be ceded by the PMG to the Navy.[9] By May 1914 there were just 19 wireless stations along the Australian and New Guinean coast.[10]

The early, dirty contests over the rights to wireless telegraphy established the close relationships between government funding, regulatory privileges, and large, politically-connected private firms that persist to this day. The Commonwealth had dealt itself into the management and operation of wireless communication with its 1905 legislation. It took a direct stake in AWA in 1921 when the government recapitalised the company so it could establish a (very expensive) direct wireless link between London and Australia. For the government, the public-private partnership gave it authority over a firm that it hoped would remain organised on commercial lines. For the AWA, Commonwealth part-ownership gave it the authority of the state and (it hoped) prevented more direct state control of the sector.[11]

These complex regulatory relationships continued with the advent of broadcasting. AWA, having first demonstrated 'broadcasting' in 1919, began experimenting with occasional broadcasts, and was joined on the air by a few amateur radio clubs dotted around the country. When AWA announced it was planning to extend these broadcasts nation-wide, the PMG stepped in (control of the spectrum had been returned to the PMG in 1920), calling a conference in 1923 to set the rules by which the Australian broadcasting industry was supposed to develop.[12]

Although it was not obvious at the time, the 1923 wireless conference established the 'Australian system' with its competitive division between public broadcasting and private broadcasting. More immediately, the conference created a peculiar and unique regulatory framework for broadcasting—the 'sealed-set' scheme—that quickly became an unworkable joke. Under this framework, listeners subscribed to individual radio stations by purchasing radio receivers that were 'sealed' by the PMG so they could only receive the stations they had subscriptions for. The sealed-set scheme was proposed and endorsed by the AWA, the most powerful industry lobby, which, as Curnow points out, was going to benefit from the equipment contracts as soon as the broadcasting framework found a stable footing.[13]

The sealed-set scheme was not much of a stable footing. Listeners quickly realised that their sets could be unsealed.[14] When the sealed-set scheme collapsed after just one year, the government established the 'open set' approach, which divided the stations into two categories. A-class stations were predominantly funded by licence fees. B-class stations were to be funded by their own efforts. While there was significant regulatory overlap—licence-fee-supported A-class stations were permitted to advertise—this system established the division between 'public' broadcasting and commercial broadcasting that was to be consolidated in 1932.[15]

The birth of public broadcasting

From its first moment, public broadcasting was driven by a fear of the consequences of private broadcasting. And for their understanding of what a private broadcasting market looked like, British and Australian policymakers fixated on the United States.

The United States was significantly ahead of the wireless technology curve. One reason for this lead was that Congress only got around to nationalising the electromagnetic spectrum in 1912. In the pre-regulatory free for all, a vibrant community of amateur radio users—'hams'—drove experimentation along. The first broadcast that did not just consist of Morse code in the United States occured as early as 1900. On Christmas Eve 1906 the Canadian-born Reginald Fessenden (a former Edison Machine Works engineer) broadcast a program consisting of a short speech, a phonograph recording of Handel's Largo, and a solo of 'O Holy Night' which Fessenden both sang and played violin, concluding with a Bible reading and a promise to broadcast again that New Year's Eve.[16] The first proper 'DJ' was Charles 'Doc' Herrold, a professor of engineering in San Jose, California, who with his students began a regular broadcast service in 1912.[17]

This lead meant that by the time Australia and the United Kingdom were trying to establish their industry structure and rules around broadcasting, the American broadcasting environment was already vibrant, innovative and, most of all, private and entrepreneurial. The United States had a proliferation of radio broadcasters—219 had been registered by May 1922—who aired religious sermons, lectures, phonograph records and live music to an audience that was 'invisible, scattered, and unknown'.[18]

By contrast, the development of radio in Britain was hesitant and uncertain. The Marconi Company only started experimenting with broadcasting in 1920, and only started regular broadcasts in January 1922. From London, the American industry looked chaotic; a jumble of broadcasters, funded by advertising, equipment sales, and donations, with stations interfering with each other on the lightly regulated spectrum. The historian Asa Briggs emphasises the shadow that this diverse private American market cast on British understandings of their own broadcasting future.[19] The future BBC director John Reith claimed that American broadcasting had 'no co-ordination, no standard, [and] no guiding policy'.[20]

Yet as the economist Thomas Hazlitt has pointed out, in practice the American broadcasting industry was far from chaotic.[21] In fact, it was governed by a common-law property rights regime. Those property rights were defined and protected by the Department of Commerce, but government intervention ended there. Spectrum rights were traded among broadcasters and the prices for spectrum rapidly increased in response to the scarcity of useful spectrum and increasing listener demand for quality programming. What the British misunderstood as 'chaos' was in fact a thriving market that facilitated the rapid growth of this new industry.

In the event, the lesson the British took from observing American broadcasting was that broadcasting needed to be controlled by the full power of the state. When the Marconi Company started its broadcasts out of the small village of Writtle in Essex, the British General Post Office (GPO) imposed heavy conditions on what could be broadcast: no music, only speech for no more than an hour a day either between 11am and 12 noon or 2pm and 4pm, interspersed with three-minute intervals in which the broadcaster was to listen for government messages.[22] These controls were soon relaxed but the relationship between regulating spectrum and regulating the speech expressed over that spectrum had been firmly established.[23]

The BBC was formed in 1922 when the GPO brought the most important companies in broadcasting (including Marconi, General Electric, and the industrial engineering firm Metropolitan-Vickers) together 'so that an efficient service may be rendered and that there may be no danger of monopoly and that each service shall not be interfering with the efficient working of the other' in the words of the Postmaster-General, Frederick Kellaway.[24] Kellaway's use of the words 'efficient' and 'monopoly' are particular to the period. Efficiency meant avoiding the apparent chaos of the American radio market. Counterposed against this was the opposite fear: that a private broadcasting network might monopolise British radio. The government and the industry agreed that the answer was a government-supported monopoly. The government and industry together created the British Broadcasting Company with exclusive broadcasting rights supported by a licence fee levied on listeners. In this way the BBC was created as an ad hoc solution to the untested fears of broadcasting monopolies and unfounded fears of broadcasting anarchy.

The romantic ideals of public broadcasting were grafted onto this political and industrial compromise after the fact.[25] The creation of the BBC had shut out a number of potential entrants to the broadcasting market. These firms, and their political allies, challenged the idea that the BBC had, in fact, been legitimately vested with a monopoly on broadcasting. The result of their agitation was the establishment of two committees of inquiry into the BBC—the Sykes committee in 1923 and the Crawford committee in 1925. But these inquiries backfired on those opposed to the public monopoly. The end result of those committees was widespread political endorsement of public control of broadcasting and the creation of the British Broadcasting Corporation in January 1927.

But what was this new BBC to do? The philosophy of public broadcasting was almost singlehandedly developed by John Reith. Reith was first appointed general manager of the BBC, and then given the inaugural Director-General role when the BBC became fully publicly owned. Reith had been an engineer with no broadcasting background when he applied for the job. Yet as early as 1923 he came to embody in the public mind what 'public broadcasting' was. Reith imbued the BBC with a sense of high moral responsibility, advocating for the BBC as a broadcaster supported by government but independent of government, with the responsibility 'to inform, to educate and to entertain' the British population. In his 1924 book Broadcast over Britain and a more straightforward submission to the Crawford Committee, Reith created the basic rationales for public broadcasting.[26] Those arguments will be examined closely in Chapter 3, but it is important to note the political and bureaucratic context for the development of those arguments: they were developed by an already established monopoly broadcaster in order to justify its own monopoly.

Public broadcasting reaches Australia

The BBC and the GPO were keen that the British dominions—at least the 'white settler' dominions of Canada, Australia, New Zealand and South Africa—draw the correct lesson from the mother country's experience. Public broadcasting on the monopoly BBC model would prevent the Americanisation of the airwaves; it would hold back crass commercialism and demagoguing radio personalities alike.[27] Between 1923 and 1939 the Director-General of Australia's PMG was Harry Brown, a former employee of the British GPO, who was in close contact with Reith and hoped to transplant the British monopoly model into Australia. The 1927 Royal Commission on Wireless heard at length from supporters and opponents of public broadcasting. Nevertheless the Royal Commission declined to recommend in its final report that the government take over broadcasting.[28]

The A-Class stations had within them the seeds of what was to become the ABC. The division between the two classes of station cemented the idea that there was something like a 'public' and a 'commercial' market. Throughout the latter half of the 1920s the Australian political class became fixated on the idea of a genuine 'national broadcasting service'. Alan Thomas identifies a number of reasons for this fixation: admiration for the principles of public broadcasting that had been articulated and apparently implemented in the United Kingdom, romantic ideals of an educated and sophisticated form of broadcasting held by Australia's small cultural elite, Country Party politicians who wanted to encourage the spread of broadcasting into rural areas, and the Labor Party which believed that commercial radio was biased against them.[29]

The ABC bill, when it was finally introduced to parliament in 1932, was the end of a process that had begun with the ill-fated sealed-set scheme. Throughout 1929 and 1930 the PMG took over the A-class stations, contracting out their programming to the Australian Broadcasting Company, a Sydney-based consortium that included one of the original Melbourne A-class stations, 3LO.[30] The Scullin Labor government—whose short and unhappy tenure during the first years of the Great Depression was characterised by the feeling that they were in a permanent state of siege against conservative interests—considered fully nationalising the entire broadcasting sector, A-class and B-class stations together. In the end they drafted a bill that would establish a Commonwealth board to control broadcasting 'on lines similar to that of the board which exists in Great Britain'.[31]

The Scullin bill was picked up by the Lyons government when it took power after the election in December 1931. While the Scullin government's interest in public broadcasting was driven by their concern about anti-Labor bias in the media and an ideological belief in nationalisation as a mode of economic control, for the Lyons government the ABC bill was an opportunity to bring some of the cultural standards of British broadcasting into Australia. As Thomas writes, Lyons 'identified with the attitudes of the Australian cultural elite who defined themselves in terms of educational and cultural levels'.[32] The Lyons government Postmaster-General, James Fenton, received a stream of delegations in January 1932 from university professors, listener groups and educationalists, emphasising the 'educational value of broadcasting, as a medium for the development of culture and public opinion ... and the need for freedom from sectional or political bias'.[33] The Australian Broadcasting Commission Bill was introduced in March 1932. When Fenton introduced the bill, he emphasised that the approach was 'as near as practicable' to the BBC model, without 'follow[ing] Great Britain slavishly'.[34] The most obvious difference was the continued existence of the B-class stations alongside the public broadcaster.

There was a bipartisan consensus on the desirability of the ABC in 1932. The historian Geoffrey Sawer remarks that Fenton 'spoke more like a Labor than a [United Australia Party] man'.[35] This meant that the parliamentary debate focused on two issues. First was the salaries of the commission, which were seen by the Labor opposition as too low to ensure that the 'right sort of first-class men' (and one woman) would be in charge. The more consequential debating point was whether the ABC would be allowed to compete for private advertising dollars. The original version of the bill stated that the ABC could accept sponsored programs. This clause was immediately the source of controversy. Newspaper associations wrote to Joseph Lyons that this clause represented 'subsidised Government interference with existing advertising channels'.[36] Faced with a backlash from media proprietors and the industry, the government backed down, inserting a clause that 'the Commission shall not broadcast advertisements'. But this displeased the Labor Party, which wanted the ABC to have the ability to attract advertisers as a check against the power and profitability of the private media. The Queensland Labor member Darby Riordan angrily attributed this new clause as 'the policy of the Melbourne *Herald* and the *Adelaide Advertiser* ... to bring about the destruction of nationalization'.[37] Nevertheless, the bill passed parliament in May 1932, and the Australian Broadcasting Commission officially opened its doors on 1 July 1932.

Nevertheless, in 1932 the ABC was just a shadow of what it was to become, producing programming that was rebroadcast by the A-class stations. The first major change to the ABC was giving it the power to create original journalism. For its first decade in operation the ABC relied on the newspapers for news-gathering that it would subsequently broadcast. Labor however claimed that this reliance meant that the biases of newspaper proprietors were being transmitted through the national broadcaster.[38] In a bill passed just before the 1946 federal election, the Chifley government required the ABC to gather its own domestic news itself. The opposition claimed that this was an attempt to bias the imminent election in the government's favour. Robert Menzies objected that the bill had been 'literally shuffled through the Parliament in the small hours of the morning on the last day of the session'.[39] Nevertheless, the bill passed parliament.

This new directive to gather news in fact represented a major shift in the purpose of the ABC, at odds with how the public broadcaster had originally been conceived. The Lyons government had been insistent that the ABC not be part of any political controversy. This went so far as declining to allow the ABC to broadcast sessions of parliament. The Lyons government's fear was not entirely unfounded: when the ABC was finally required to broadcast parliament in June 1946, it was immediately met by demands from politicians demanding right-of-reply when they were criticised in broadcast sessions. The audience did not welcome the parliamentary broadcasts: one listener complained that 'someone should enlighten interjectors that their pearls of wit are unintelligible over the air and come through as boorish and uncouth grunts and shouts'.[40] These broadcasts notwithstanding, amendments made a few years later to broadcasting legislation prohibited the ABC from discussing any political controversy more recent than five years old.[41]

News-gathering also represented a significant new burden on the ABC's finances. The ABC was funded from a combination of licence fees and top-up funding from the government, a financial structure which could be traced back to the sealed-set scheme. The ABC lobbied for an increase in licence fees to cover these additional costs.[42] The request sparked a serious internal discussion in the Chifley government in 1948 about whether to nationalise the entire broadcasting industry. This would have been in keeping with that government's radically democratic-socialist policy program, which included nationalising the airlines and the banks.[43] In the end the Chifley government decided to eliminate the licence fee and fund the entire service from general government expenditure. Ken Inglis shows that the immediate result was a boost in funding for the public broadcaster. But this boost was a double-edged sword.[44] Now the ABC had to come directly to the government to finance its expenditure. Licence fees by contrast were one more step removed from the government and offered the ABC greater independence.

The ABC acquires television

The introduction of television was another pivotal moment in the development of public broadcasting. The question of whether Australia should adopt the British monopoly model or the American private competition model had to be debated once again. It was not obvious at the time that the hybrid structure developed for radio broadcasting would be extended to the new technology. In that sense the debates over the introduction of television saw many of the rationales for the existence of the ABC either reiterated or reorientated. But this time the ABC was an incumbent bureaucracy with an interest in extending its power and control.

The global adoption of television had been slowed by the Second World War. The Scottish engineer John Logie Baird first demonstrated the wireless broadcast of moving pictures to a group of about forty members of the Royal Institution in London in 1926—so many that they had to file in to see the demonstration in batches of six at a time.[45] The BBC began its first regular television broadcasting in November 1936—two hours a day excluding Sundays. The technology was being rolled out when it was suddenly stopped by the outbreak of war in Europe. The British government could not justify the resources that television required—in terms of skilled engineers, the industry to produce television sets, or the spectrum now being demanded for military purposes. Once the war was over, the pressure on resources did not disappear. The need for rebuilding, and the era of austerity it engendered, meant that the resumption and diffusion of television was slow.

The Australian government was well informed about the introduction of television in Britain. Some of Baird's television equipment made its way to Australia in the late 1920s, and in 1932 Australia participated in experiments with international broadcasting.[46] The Postmaster-General James Fenton was positively giddy about the future prospects of television when he was introducing the ABC Bill in 1932, having seen early experiments demonstrated at 10 Downing Street on a visit to London. While the 1932 legislation made no provision for television broadcasting, Fenton reassured his parliamentary colleagues that 'it is unlikely that the proposed broadcasting commission would overlook any great developments in television'.[47] The 1941 Joint Parliamentary Committee into Wireless heard from a range of witnesses about the exciting possibilities of television but concluded that 'much development is necessary before its introduction should be authorized'.[48]

British television broadcasts resumed in 1946. It took the Chifley government another two years to reach a conclusion about how the new service should be run in Australia. At one stage the government said that no television service could be rolled out until every Australian had a telephone service.[49] In the end Labor's decision was consistent with their economic philosophy: television should be provided by a monopoly national provider. Ben Chifley declared that the government's interest was in preventing the commercial monopolisation of the service, given that the high costs of broadcasting would push smaller commercial operators out of the market.[50] Whether that monopoly provider was to be the ABC was still an open question when Labor lost the election to Robert Menzies in December 1949.[51]

The Menzies government was not much more enthusiastic about television. At one of the first cabinet meetings in February 1950, the new Postmaster General, Larry Anthony, stated that the new technology would be 'a very cogent social force' and 'must therefore be carefully and soundly developed'.[52] The Menzies government early on resolved to extend the hybrid structure onto television, allowing for a national broadcaster and one commercial licence in each capital. Yet this decision was no spark for action. Ken Inglis notes that there was little pressure to bring television forward. Both newspaper and radio broadcast interests were concerned about the competition and (if they planned to enter the market) the cost. The only advocates were those who wished to make and sell television equipment.[53] The result of this delay was that Australian consumers were denied television for two decades after it had been introduced in the United Kingdom—a longstanding theme in the history of Australian media policy, as incumbent industries have lobbied to keep technologies like television, FM radio and cable television from undercutting their markets.[54]

In 1953, Menzies handed the television question over to a Royal Commission. The Royal Commission heard about all manner of harms that television might inflict upon the Australian population—that it was psychologically damaging, would reduce reading, encouraged 'mediocrity and vulgar sensationalism', and would be a 'very effective weapon for propaganda'.[55] A series of witnesses either called for television to be delayed, to be heavily censored, or for commercial interests to be prohibited from entering the market. The ABC was one of those interested party in the television debate. Richard Boyer, who had been the chair of the ABC since 1945, was eager to convince the Royal Commission that radio broadcasts and television broadcasts were qualitatively different:

> There is a primitive element in sight which seems to go deeper and be more critical in its effect than sound can ever be ... This consideration introduces a further element inherent in a visual medium as opposed to oral, which is engaging the attention of sociologists, namely, that sight in addition to being the most intense of the avenues of consciousness is probably also the most primitive.[56]

This the ABC believed was good reason to slow or delay the introduction of television; a recommendation which the Royal Commission ultimately gave: 'television should be introduced on a gradual basis'.

The first proper Australian television broadcasts occurred in 1956 (although there were numerous experimental broadcasts before that).[57] The introduction of television simply continued the hybrid public-private structure established two decades earlier. Nevertheless, the decision to simultaneously introduce commercial and public television in Australia should be seen as significant. The journalist Sandra Hall wrote that the decision 'doomed the ABC as a tastemaker'.[58] The historian Ann Curthoys notes that it allowed TV to 'develop more freely' than if the ABC had a monopoly; helping create the Australian culture that 'is distinctive, not in being unique or entirely "new", but in always negotiating between, rejecting, modifying, adding to, changing, and transforming, British and American cultural forms and arguments'.[59]

A 'corporate' ABC

The ABC was fifty years old when it was restructured by the Australian Broadcasting Corporation Act 1983, which also renamed it from a 'Commission' to a 'Corporation'. The reform package was intended to give the ABC a clearer purpose and direction. This package originated in a 1976 committee of inquiry into the overall structure of the Australian broadcasting industry, which, in response to complaints and ongoing industrial turmoil at the ABC, had recommended regular reviews be held into the ABC's performance.[60] The first of these reviews was commissioned by the Fraser government. Tony Staley, the Minister for Posts and Telecommunications, told the cabinet that

> a major factor leading to unrest in the ABC has been the different interpretations of the statutory role of the commission, and consequently about the level of resources needed to enable the Commission to discharge its responsibilities. The Broadcasting and Television Act 1942 expresses the ABC's role in broad terms only, and commercial broadcasters, members of the public and the ABC itself place varying, and sometimes conflicting, interpretations on such statutory expressions as the requirement that the Commission provide 'adequate and comprehensive programs'.[61]

That review, headed up by Alex Dix, who was managing director of the consumer goods company Reckitt and Colman, is the most comprehensive investigation into the ABC in the public broadcaster's history. Released in 1981, it is also the only inquiry to seriously evaluate the purpose of public broadcasting.

Yet the Dix inquiry had a notable analytical weakness. Asking directly 'Do we need an ABC?' it answered positively, 'We know that most Australians want a National Broadcasting Service', then went on to detail a number of population surveys which supported this statement.[62] From the surveys it drew out a conclusion that the ABC should not present itself as a niche or specialised broadcaster, filling in segments of the market which commercial broadcasters had failed to. Rather, a survey commissioned for the Dix inquiry found that 'By a factor of about five to one, the feeling that the ABC should provide programs for the general community rather than for those sections of the community that the commercial stations don't cater for is dominant'.[63]

Yet audience surveys are a thin foundation on which to mount an argument for public broadcasting. While such information tells policymakers what they would like, it provides only limited information for policy setting. Any policy framework has trade-offs, including the taxation burden and indirect costs on the rest of the sector. The Dix inquiry argued that the ABC needed clearer direction about what it should do—yet that direction was not developed by an analysis of the need for the ABC, but by surveys which considered the popularity of the ABC. The two are not the same thing. Nevertheless, the Dix inquiry took the survey preferences and sought to construct a rationale for the ABC around it.

The conceptual incoherence that resulted from this approach undermined the otherwise laudable goal of providing clearer direction to the ABC. It recommended that the ABC be given a Charter that would guide its programming decisions. ABC content should be 'informative, entertaining, innovative, and directed towards Australian society as a whole, and to its constituent community groups'.[64] When this recommendation was converted into statute, it became the modern Charter, with its insistence that the ABC inform, entertain, and contribute to a sense of national identity. Criticism that ABC content did not reflect Australian multiculturalism also led to a requirement that the ABC 'reflect the cultural diversity of the Australian community'. The 1983 legislation also made a series of structural reforms to the ABC, including severing ABC employees from the Public Service Board. This was done in response to complaints that the ABC was unable to compete with commercial broadcasters for staff, given the strictures around public service employment.

More than three decades later it is clear that the 1983 reforms did little to structure the ABC's purpose and direction. Corporatisation was the last major reform to the ABC. Subsequent significant reviews have only addressed the question of the aim of public broadcasting slightly or tangentially. A departmental review in 1988 recommended that there be a clearer distinction between Charter and non-Charter activities.[65] But this recommendation was not adopted by the government. A Senate Committee report in 1995 recommended some minor changes to the ABC's accountability and financial accounting.[66]

The Howard government took a more direct approach to the ABC. Shortly after the 1996 election it commissioned business leader Bob Mansfield to investigate the ABC's purpose, including taking into account the 'anticipated technological change affecting broadcasting services'. By the mid-1990s the revolutionary character of digital media was becoming evident, and parliament was starting to concern itself with how the internet would affect policy areas like tax and copyright. Nevertheless, these technological changes led to little rethinking of the purpose of public broadcasting, and for the most part the Mansfield review reads as an update to the Dix review. While recommending that the Charter be amended to provide more clarity—for example, to specify that the ABC ought to provide an independent news service—it endorsed the position that the ABC should not try to be a 'complementary' broadcaster, filling in the gaps of the commercial media. Yet at the same time the Mansfield review also rejected the suggestion that it be a 'comprehensive' broadcaster, trying to please all Australian communities at the same time. The ABC ought not to compete with commercial broadcasters, but it should take their content offerings into account.[67]

Unsurprisingly, as this confusing attempt to thread a needle suggests, the Mansfield review failed to clearly define the policy goals of the ABC. That left the Mansfield review unable to fully engage with some of the more dramatic proposals it considered. For example, the review considered, and rejected, the possibility that public broadcasting funding could be contestable—that is, public interest programming could be tendered out to competitive broadcasters. This, the Mansfield review concluded, would undermine the ABC's independence and its ability to conduct long-term planning. Like the Dix review, and each inquiry before it, the Mansfield review skated over the fundamental policy question in public broadcasting. It is time to ask: what is the ABC for?

3 Why does the public need a broadcaster?

In his classic study of the regulation of television in the United States, the economist Harvey J. Levin wrote that 'the stated purposes of federal broadcast licensing ... can quite properly serve as a major yardstick by which to evaluate its end results'.[1] But Australians looking for a clear and unadorned statement of the need for public broadcasting and the policy goals of the ABC will be engaged on a fruitless search. The Charter offers no guide. The ABC was established in 1932 but its character and direction took decades to establish. The ministers who introduced the Australian Broadcasting Commission Bill 1932 and the Australian Broadcasting Corporation Bill 1983 respectively did not outline what they believed the policy rationale for the ABC was. Recent major inquiries, like the Dix and Mansfield reviews, were also reluctant to directly spell out the ABC's purpose, preferring to tackle tangential questions.

Nevertheless, it is possible to uncover a set of rationales for public broadcasting, both generally and in Australia, in the inquiries, in the parliamentary debates, and in the controversies which have swirled around the ABC. In this chapter we identify eight key policy justifications for the existence of the ABC, used at various times throughout its history: that public broadcasting is needed a) to resolve a market failure in the broadcasting market, b) to increase pluralism and diversity in the Australian media market, c) as an independent counterbalance to media owned by commercial moguls, d) to ensure quality broadcasting, e) to paternalistically raise tastes and standards, f) to ensure rural citizens have access to media, g) to subsidise Australian culture, and h) to provide information to citizens about their democracy. These arguments can be seen as the disorder costs of the market provision of media and broadcasting.

One question is the relative weight we should give these arguments. Throughout its long history, the ABC has explicitly rejected some justifications and has downplayed others. For example, explicitly paternalistic arguments for public broadcasting were common during the first decades of the ABC, but do not appear in more recent formulations of the role of public broadcasting. Even so, paternalism can be said to permeate other arguments. What the Mansfield review described as the divide between the ABC's complementary and comprehensive missions is in fact a modern reformulation of a more clearly paternalistic rationale described in the ABC's first annual report:

> Enlightenment must come through entertainment. The Commission therefore aims to develop side by side its two ideals of pleasing and benefiting, and this it hopes to do by continually striving to render its service pleasing and its pleasing serviceable; it will seek to appeal not to each section of the community in turn, but to all sections at all times.[2]

Ambiguity in a bureaucratic mission serves the interests of that bureaucracy.[3] But it does not necessarily serve the public interest. As we shall see, the ABC has long resisted too much mission clarity. In the following sections we examine the arguments for public broadcasting, and show how they are either anachronistic, illiberal, or can be achieved more efficiently and cheaply through other means.

Market failure

The standard economic rationale for government intervention in the economy is market failure. Market failures occur when the outcomes of a competitive market are inefficient. This is a technical concept which leans on a specific definition of inefficiency—where it is possible to reallocate resources that would make at least one person better off without making anyone else worse off. In popular debate however the phrase 'market failure' is used much more loosely, describing any result of a market that fails to live up to the 'public interest', however that is defined. Broadcasting markets might be susceptible to market failure in a number of ways.[4]

The first is that both media products and media content can have the attributes of a public good. A lot of people think of the services provided by the ABC as being a 'public good'.[5] By that they usually mean a good provided by the government on behalf of the public. People also tend to think of schools and hospitals and the like in the same terms. Other times people think of public goods as being those things that are good for the public. Economists, however, have a somewhat different definition of public goods. To qualify as a public good the good or service must be both 'non-excludable' and 'non-rival'. So nobody can stop anyone from using a particular good or service and prior use of the good or service doesn't prevent others from using it too. There are remarkably few goods and services that actually meet those criteria. Remember, to qualify as a public good both conditions must be met. National security and the rule of law are usually held out as examples of public goods. Public broadcasting, however, may be good for the public, but it isn't a public good.

Of course, this technical quibbling shouldn't be the end of the discussion. Adam Smith had a less technical and more intuitive definition of public good. Those goods and services:

> ... which, though they may be in the highest degree advantageous to a great society, are, however, of such a nature that the profit could never repay the expense to any individual or small number of individuals, and which it therefore cannot be expected that any individual or small number of individuals should erect or maintain.[6]

That suggests a two-pronged test; a public good must be advantageous to a great society but must be inherently unprofitable. Note there is a difference between being a non-profit organisation and being inherently unprofitable. The ABC is the former but, perhaps, not the latter. No doubt there are many who would argue that the ABC passes the 'advantageous to a great society' test. That case, however, must be proven, and not just asserted or assumed.

An alternative market failure can exist if economies of scale and scope tend towards a natural monopoly. Media markets are susceptible to this as well: all the cost of producing content occurs when producing the first 'unit' of content, and subsequent units are either costless or close to costless. Without the pressure of competition, natural monopolies can lead to higher costs and worse goods and services.

A third market failure concerns externalities, where market transactions have either a positive or negative impact on people who are not direct participants in the transaction. If those externalities are negative, economists worry that the third parties have not been compensated. If those externalities are positive, they worry that the goods or services in question will be undersupplied. The most typical example of an externality used in the context of media control is a positive externality created by high quality content: more consumption of Shakespeare's plays will lead to a more educated and refined society that benefits even by those who did not directly consume the extra Shakespeare.

Standard economic analysis says that governments should intervene to fix these failures: taxing or regulating negative externalities, regulating so that firms do not monopolise, and subsidising or directly providing goods which generate positive externalities or are public goods. Public broadcasting might have a role to play in each of these instances. The original British model of public monopolisation was intended to reduce negative externalities of broadcasting by nationalisation. In Australia's hybrid system, public broadcasters can provide competitive pressure to prevent the emergence of a commercial monopoly. In addition, public broadcasters can directly provide public goods and goods with positive externalities.

As an independent review of the BBC concluded in 1999:

> ... some form of market failure must lie at the heart of any concept of public service broadcasting. Beyond simply using the catch-phrase that public service broadcasting must 'inform, educate and entertain', we must add 'inform, educate and entertain in a way which the private sector, left unregulated, would not do'. Otherwise, why not leave matters entirely to the private sector?[7]

Yet does the ABC exist to resolve market failures in broadcasting? The ABC has itself given mixed answers. Mark Scott, director of the ABC between 2006 and 2016, claimed that the choices the ABC made to enter or extend itself into certain areas of content were driven by a belief that they were being undersupplied by commercial networks. In an interview with the Guardian in 2011 as director, Scott described it as 'market failure broadcaster', and rationalised the ABC's expanding offerings as due to the fact that 'the areas of market failure are getting greater'.[8] However, a spokesperson for Scott later backed away from the language of market failure.[9]

Scott's successor, the former Google executive Michelle Guthrie, has forcefully rejected the claim that the ABC is a market failure broadcaster.[10] A parliamentary submission by the ABC in 2016 (while Scott was still ABC director) argued that:

> Despite claims to the contrary, the ABC has never been, and nor will it ever be, a 'market failure broadcaster.' It was created alongside commercial broadcasters in the 1930s to provide a range of quality programming and to maximise diversity within the Australian media sector.[11]

The Charter provides little guide. It requires the ABC to 'take account of' the activities of commercial and community broadcasters but says nothing about what the ABC should do in response. The former ABC chair, James Spigelman, has argued that in fact 'it would be illegal for [the ABC] to become a market failure broadcaster because we are required to balance programs of general appeal and special appeal'.[12] This significantly overstates the enforceability and legal character of the ABC's Charter. More fundamentally, the language of the Charter does not preclude market failure broadcasting—to the extent that the market for media fails, it does so not simply because it does not feed niche interests but because general interests are not sufficiently supplied. Ironically, these passionate rejections of the market failure argument by ABC management in fact significantly understate the strength of the economic argument for public broadcasting.

The history of the ABC does, in fact, suggest that public broadcasting in Australia has been conceived through a market failure lens. The basic problem for radio in the 1920s was how to fund broadcasting. Policymakers assumed that the only way to pay for this new technology was through licence fees and equipment sales. Their solution was first the sealed-set scheme, then the creation of the A-class stations. The advertising-supported B-class stations were an afterthought; a concession to those who lobbied to experiment with the new medium as a purely commercial practice. While subsequent decades demonstrated that advertising was an effective mechanism for funding commercial radio, and then television, the early uncertainty about this is understandable. Given that the A-class stations were nationalised over the next decade and grouped into the ABC, it is reasonable to say that the ABC was, originally, at least in one significant way, introduced to fix a market failure in broadcasting.

Yet is there a role for the ABC in fixing market failures today? Just as the technological and economic environment is substantially different compared to the early 1930s, the structure of potential market failures in the media also is substantially different. It is certainly the case that established business models have struggled in recent years due to the unbundling of classified advertising from journalism. As we write this, it seems very likely that both Melbourne and Sydney will become one-newspaper towns, as already are Perth, Brisbane, Canberra, Hobart and Adelaide. But there has also been massive entry into media content markets—the extreme abundance of digital content has in fact created the dire circumstances which the traditional newspapers find themselves in.

Claims that any given market is 'monopolised' are highly dependent on the definition of the market. This is particularly the case for industries undergoing rapid technological change. As the economists Christopher Pleatsikas and David Teece write, 'there are periodic, unpredictable and discontinuous paradigm shifts that can completely undermine incumbents using existing dominant technologies. Such shifts can and do often result in a total change in the competitive positions in the industry'.[13] While the market for 'newspapers' seems to be tending towards monopoly, the market for media content has never been more vibrant. Indeed, the fears of broadcasting monopolisation in the 1920s or 1950s might have been eased if broadcasting had been seen as an economic competitor to newspapers. The overwrought concerns about television-watching displacing novel-reading aired in the

Royal Commission on Television could have been seen as an economic argument about competition, not just an aesthetic one.

While fears of natural monopoly must certainly have eased since the ABC's creation, media content retains its public good characteristics. Yet here too technological change has substantially changed the economic dynamic. When the ABC was established it was impossible to prevent listeners from tuning into a station without paying for it—hence the ill-fated sealed-set scheme. The solution at the time to this problem was the creation of advertising markets. Since the advent of subscription television, technological change now allows content providers to prevent users who have not paid from accessing content—taking away one of the key planks of public goods, their non-excludability. Encryption and rights management software allows for excludability on the internet. While paywalls can be bypassed and content pirated, digital distribution networks for music and streaming services are demonstrating that any public good characteristics of music content can be amply compensated through innovation.[14]

The positive externalities of some media content have not been restructured by technological change. Later in this chapter we tackle the special instance of journalism in a democratic context, which is under particular pressure as its traditional financial foundations are ripped apart. For now it is important to recognise that the accessibility of 'quality' media content has never been higher. The globalisation of media content has opened up vast new avenues through which the highest quality content can be delivered. Ivy League universities offer lectures for their courses free online. Private self-education providers like the Great Courses offer hundreds of high quality but affordable programs from top-level professors.[15] Streaming services like Netflix, Stan and Spotify give users a choice of both high-brow and low-brow content, as easily accessible as each other. In this new context, it is not at all clear that the market provision of media content is underproviding media content with positive externalities.

More fundamentally however, even if the ABC were to embrace an identity as a market failure organisation, this would leave a large number of policy questions unanswered. It is common to assume that the identification of a market failure is sufficient reason for government intervention. But successful government intervention is easier to imagine than implement. While markets can 'fail', governments can fail too. As Friedrich Hayek pointed out, governments usually lack the necessary information to make the sort of fine-grained adjustments to market processes that theories of market failure intervention demand.[16] While media markets have some characteristics of public good and positive externalities, the question policymakers have to answer is not whether they should intervene, but how much and in what manner. Too much intervention is just as much a 'failure' as too little. The economists Christopher Coyne and Peter Leeson ask 'how will government officials know the level of the subsidy or to whom to give the subsidy?'[17] The diffuse and unspecified consequences of market failures in a media market make this problem even more difficult. It is not at all clear that public broadcasting is the appropriate solution to market failure in media, even in the absence of the technology revolution of the last two decades.

Cultural diversity

Even if media markets do not fail in a technical economic sense, they might function in a way contrary to the (vaguely defined) public interest, and this might offer reasons for more state control of broadcasting and the media in general. One of the most common complaints about the broadcast media since its formation is its apparent tendency to supply content almost exclusively for the median listener or viewer. Public broadcasting could provide cultural pluralism and diversity that commercial broadcasting may not be able to support. The diversity of programming has long been a focus of regulators around the world. Harvey Levin considers program diversity—that is, diversity of broadcasting programs across both type and timeslot—as a 'merit good' and supports government intervention to ensure merit programming is broadcast.[18] (The word 'diversity' here refers to a general spread of content across genres, audiences, and interests.) The communications theorist Denis McQuail argues that diversity fosters 'innovation, creativity and originality' and 'contributes to social order by promoting free expression of discontent or disagreement and by offering pathways to compromise'.[19] Thus, while a lack of diversity might not be technically a market failure, it could be socially suboptimal.

The ABC is required through its Charter to 'reflect the cultural diversity of the Australian community'. In context this requirement is narrower than the program diversity notion discussed by Levin, and was explicitly introduced as part of the 1983 reforms to enhance the ABC's multicultural role. Nonetheless the ABC believes that one of its core roles is to 'maximise diversity'—which, as we have seen, it distinguishes from a market failure role. The Mansfield review predicted that while new digital technologies were likely to boost program diversity, that new diversity, however, would probably be 'low cost content ... and packages of services with minimal commentary, added value or distinctive flavour'. The ABC would continue to have a role in producing and distributing content with 'an Australian viewpoint' and which covered 'issues of interest to Australians'.[20] This is also seen by supporters of the ABC as a critical function of public broadcasting.[21]

The idea that media markets might lack diversity has its origins in a famous spatial economic model by the mathematical economist Harold Hotelling. He mapped out how firms acted in relation to each other. In his famous model, a market with a small number of firms that is not competing on price will offer near identical products. Hotelling believed this explained the 'excessive sameness' in capitalist markets.[22] For most of the twentieth century the Hotelling principle of minimum product differentiation has been widely understood to describe real world broadcasting markets.[23] A standard explanation is offered in the *Handbook on the Digital Creative Economy*:

> [S]tations based on advertising revenue will seek to maximize their audience (and thereby their revenue). Stations will therefore duplicate programme types as long as the audience share obtained is greater than that from other programmes. Hence a number of stations may compete by sharing a market for one type of programme (such as crime dramas) and still do better in audience numbers than by providing programmes of other types (such as arts and culture).[24]

Yet the media policy relevance of the Hotelling model of excessive sameness was questionable from its first moment. It offers no explanation for the emergence of public broadcasting. Hotelling's paper was published in 1929, seven years after the BBC was formed as a monopoly to reduce the diversity—that is, the cacophony and anarchy—of radio broadcasting seen in the United States. Nor was it a useful description of the media even in the 1920s and 1930s. The original model was structured around a duopoly, but media markets have never been duopolies: even in one and two-newspaper towns, alternative formats of media content compete with each other. Radio, motion pictures, newspapers, books and (when it arrived) television all competed for the same entertainment and news space, and many of them competing on price.

A similar historical problem with the Hotelling argument for public broadcasting is that having only a small number of firms in the broadcasting market is a policy choice. Broadcasting markets have been structured less by the inherent economic attributes of broadcasting and more by the politics of spectrum allocation. The Wireless Telegraphy Act gave the Australian government power over entry to broadcasting, which it has wielded strongly in favour of protecting incumbent broadcasters. Australian governments have long known that many more services could be delivered on the existing spectrum. The 1942 parliamentary inquiry into wireless was told that with some amendment to the radio frequency plan, 'several hundred' channels could be allocated across Australia.[25] The long-running saga about whether to introduce a fourth commercial television network was based not on spectrum scarcity but on claims that more competition would harm the financial viability of the incumbent broadcasters.[26] The introduction of subscription television was first recommended by the Australian Broadcasting Tribunal in 1982, but its introduction was delayed until 1995.[27] (That delay is particularly significant as subscription television introduces price competition, which complicates the Hotelling model.) As Franco Papandrea writes, 'the history of Australian broadcasting is littered with examples of costly mistakes by governments intent on protecting the private interests of established broadcasters with little consideration of market forces and consumer demand'.[28]

Spatial theories of media diversity are deeply influential and well-known. But their policy relevance is questionable when transcribed from a world of two media outlets to the world of the internet. With online media, the number of firms and the variety of content they can offer is functionally infinite. While clustering may still occur, the limitless spread of content makes it hard to see how the diversity could be less than socially optimal. In the context of media diversity, Hotelling models, the economist Gillian Doyle writes, 'begin to fail when direct charges to the viewer, multiple sellers and competition based on prices are introduced'.[29] Unless socially suboptimal diversity is defined as the distribution of media content in a market that lacks a public broadcaster, then virtually limitless niche content online should satisfy this policy requirement. If public broadcasting is meant to resolve the problem that the market provision of media offers less diversity that is socially optimal, then it has no place in the digital age.

Independence

The Charter describes the ABC as an 'independent national broadcasting service', and it is that independence which forms many arguments in favour of public broadcasting. But this notion of independence needs deeper examination. The ABC is a state-owned broadcaster, which is dependent on triennial funding arrangements drawn from the Commonwealth budget, which is set by the political discretion of the government of the day. ABC supporters refer to the ABC's independence in two senses. First, it has editorial independence from the government, insofar as it is a statutory agency that is self-managing and separated from the normal chains of political accountability. Second, it is independent of the interests of advertisers and private sector media moguls, providing the 'independent information' that the commercial media might not.[30]

Public broadcasting has always been defined against the evils of private broadcasting, and the theme of an independent bulwark against the commercial media (the moguls and monopolists) has been integral right from the start. We have seen the claims made in the early years that a purely private media market would be simultaneously disorderly and monopolistic. In the debate over the 1932 bill, the Labor member for Kalgoorlie, Albert Green, warned of the 'chains of newspapers ... obtaining such a stranglehold over the eastern part of the Victoria, and disseminating its propaganda through the stations that it controls'.[31] The private monopolisation of radio—'one of the most revolutionary additions to the pool of human resources'—was constantly invoked by Labor members throughout the early debates.[32] This concern, they felt, was more than just theoretical. The 1931 election loss showed, they felt, that the private media was systematically biased against the Labor Party, and a public broadcaster would be able to right that wrong.[33]

Control of the wireless was the high ground of the political contest during the interwar years. In New South Wales the Lang government had sought to establish a state government radio network that would resist what Labor saw as the Nationalist Party-dominated private media.[34] As Green, the most forthright of the Labor members on this point in the 1932 debate, put it:

> Some B class stations are controlled by newspaper combines, which use them to broadcast only one political opinion. I had hoped that the air would be free to all, and that at election time every party would be given an opportunity to express its opinions over the air. Unfortunately that has not been our experience. Certain newspaper combines are endeavouring to obtain a monopoly of B class stations, and I sound the note of warning that sooner or later some government will have to tackle the very difficult, but necessary task of dealing with the problem of metropolitan B class stations. Nothing short of a complete national scheme will do.[35]

In this sense, independence was understood by the Labor Party as being pro-Labor—or, at least, not anti-Labor. The 1942 inquiry into wireless reiterated this concern, arguing that public broadcasting was needed 'to prevent the service from being used for improper purposes'.[36]

Similar concerns drove the introduction of television. The overwrought claims about the social and psychological power of television only intensified the concerns about the new technology's political importance. As Ann Curthoys shows, the public position of the Labor Party and the ACTU emphasised the cultural good that public broadcasting television could bring, rather than its role countering political bias. But there is no doubt that politics was front of mind when the labour movement considered the significance of television. A public disagreement between Arthur Calwell and H.V. Evatt as to whether Labor would nationalise the commercial television stations if they were returned to government pivoted on their different impressions of how sympathetic the ABC was to the Labor Party. Calwell, who had been Minister for Information during the Second World War, had a hostile relationship to the commercial press. He believed that Keith Murdoch, who owned the Melbourne *Herald* and several other papers across the country, was 'a fifth columnist', 'megalomanic', and his network of papers 'a law unto itself' and 'Public Enemy No. 1 of the liberties of the Australian people'.[37] Murdoch's pernicious influence could not be let onto television. Evatt felt that if the hybrid system was maintained, at least the Labor Party would be able to buy a commercial station to air its views.[38] For its part, the conservative parties were just as aware of the political significance of television, arguing in response to the Chifley government's proposal to establish a monopoly broadcaster that Labor was 'merely another milestone on the socialised road to serfdom'.[39]

The modern ABC's independence is often declared but its substance is hard to pin down. Unlike the BBC, the ABC was not established under a royal charter, and the 1948 move away from licence fees to funding through budget appropriations brought it more into the political window. As Inglis shows throughout his two-volume history, the move towards what is now seen as the ABC's independence was evolutionary and halting, and even now ABC independence is hardly secure.[40]

Yet how independent could the ABC be? Compared to private and non-government organisations, the fortune of any state authority is going to be closely tied to the government of the day. Public broadcasters have their budgets set by the same governments which they purport to keep a check on. Commercial broadcasters might be dependent on the goodwill of advertisers, but the fact that there are many potential advertisers is a protection against excessive advertiser influence. A public broadcaster has only one funder, and it is a funder whose interests are driven by political rather than commercial imperatives.

Nor are commercial broadcasters required to constantly justify their activities to professional politicians. Public broadcasters are regularly brought in front of parliamentary committees to answer for editorial decisions, from the trivial to the significant. The Senate Estimates committee procedure requires statutory agencies to present themselves in front of a committee of Senators three times a year. At her first Senate estimates hearing in May 2016, Michelle Guthrie was interrogated about the cancelation of livestock market reports on ABC regional stations, the ABC Fact Check program, how unionised the ABC's workforce was, whether the ABC was too Sydney-centric, how many people it sent to the Cannes film festival and how long they were out of the office, and how much the ABC spent on a custom typeface to use across its brands.[41] This sort of scrutiny is, of course, entirely appropriate for a state instrumentality. But it is hard to watch these sorts of hearings and argue that the ABC's unique value as a media outlet is its independence.

Nonetheless, it is not obvious that having such a large government body 'independent' from a democratically elected government is desirable. The ABC is a state-owned organisation, and like any state-owned organisation it derives its legitimacy from its relationship to the democratic expression of voter preferences. Public broadcasters join a large number of other regulatory and bureaucratic agencies that have been deliberately separated from the normal lines of democratic accountability: rather than being the 'arm of the minister', in the classical Westminster bureaucracy formulation, they are protected from political interference and given independence.[42] In an open market, private media organisations are subordinate to consumers and advertisers. In government, politicians and bureaucracies are subordinate to voters. Independent statutory agencies are, by intention, subordinate to neither. Even at their most benign, they are highly susceptible to capture by their employees and management.

Indeed, staff capture has been a longstanding concern of critics of public broadcasters. As Michael Warby writes, '"Independence" from government interference … comes to mean effective independence from whatever tenuous public controls over the ABC exist in practice—it amounts to independence from the direct legal owner'.[43] An evocative description of the BBC in its early years by one of its employees describes a more general problem of independent public broadcasting:

> The atmosphere was one-third boarding school, one-third Chelsea party, one-third crusade. Or possibly the crusade bulked a little larger. There was the same feeling of dedication and hope which had characterised the League of Nations in its earliest days …
>
> The elemental fact about broadcasting is its tremendous output. You may have all the authorities and restrictions and committees and regulations: but they are all defeated by the

> rapidity of successive programmes ... in the last resort public opinion will be formed by the men who actually produce programmes. The men who sit at the top, the ageing generals, the chairmen of gas boards, the ineffective professors, the uninspired journalists ... know almost nothing about what is going on under their noses.[44]

In Chapter 4 we detail one of the consequences of staff capture—political bias. The historical context shows that this political slant is a deliberate feature of public broadcasting, not a bug.

It is certainly true that the notion that the ABC needs to be an independent, objective, unbiased, political neutral counterbalance to the commercial and non-profit media providers has a firm hold on the idea of public broadcasting. The ABC's editorial director wrote in 2015 that 'being objective' was a discipline to which the ABC was committed, counterpoised against the 'information presented to us by those with hidden agendas, causes to push and products to sell'.[45] The ABC is still presented by its defenders as a bulwark against media 'moguls' and the media landscape depicted as a contest between commercial-political powerhouses and the independent, publicly owned press.[46]

How relevant is this vision of the media in the twenty-first century? Media moguls have never had less power—both direct political power and diffuse, cultural power—than they do today. The influence of News Corp's Rupert Murdoch pales in comparison to the sway that the newspaper barons of the past held over governments and nations. Historically, newspaper editors and media owners have not been shy in proclaiming their power. The Victorian-era British newspaper and magazine editor W.T. Stead declared the beginning of 'government by journalism' in 1886, arguing that the press had replaced the House of Commons as the 'Chamber of Initiative ... [n]o measure ever gets itself into shape, as a rule, before being debated many times as a project in the columns of the newspapers'.[47] When Stead perished on the *Titanic*, his iconic status as a mogul was taken over by the American press tycoon William Randolph Hearst (the tycoon portrayed in Orson Welles' film *Citizen Kane* as able to declare wars and break governments) and Lord Beaverbrook, who described his jewel the *Daily Express* as existing 'merely for the purposes of making propaganda and with no other motive'.[48]

It is doubtful these tycoons ever commanded the power they proclaimed. Nevertheless, to the extent that they did hold that sway, the mechanisms with which they were able to do so simply do not apply any more. The mogul who imposes their views on their newspaper would be much more influential if they held a monopoly or near-monopoly over the press than when they compete in a media environment characterised by abundance. As Eli Noam writes, 'The fewer choices, the greater their economic power. The fewer voices, the greater their political and idea power'.[49] But even the most hyperventilating claims about Rupert Murdoch's influence cannot avoid the fact that critics of News Corp have more outlets for their critiques than ever before in history, and social media provides a historically unparalleled mechanism for distributing those critiques. Likewise, the globalisation of the media market through the internet means that media concentration ought to be considered in a global context.[50]

Other factors have undermined the power of the mogul as well. One structural change over the last few decades has been the move from family-owned firms to publicly-owned companies—often with large shares held by institutional investors—which directs media companies to focus more on profit than diffuse notions of political power. The media economist Benjamin Compaine finds that '[p]ublicly owned newspaper chains are less likely to have an ideological agenda they want to promote than those that are family controlled'.[51] Furthermore, increased consolidation is not a synonym for increased control—more media properties make it harder for a mogul to distribute and police their personal political preferences across their outlets, rather than easier. Counterintuitively, large conglomerates empower editors rather than owners.[52]

It ought to be harder than ever to argue the case for public broadcasting on the grounds that it is a bulwark against media monopolisation. Yet it appears that this concern is as prevalent as ever. Adam Thierer asks a provocative question: 'Could it be that what media critics really fear is not a concentration of corporate ownership but a concentration of consumer tastes?'[53] This question goes to the heart of the next two arguments for public broadcasting: quality and paternalism.

Quality

If public broadcasting is intended to provide both diversity and independence, it is important to realise a diverse media does not necessary mean a media characterised by 'quality', however defined. One media critic noted the typically one-sided uses of the concept of diversity in discussions about the media:

> What ... diversity is never really gets defined, but readers may be left with the suspicion that there is a particular view-

> point they feel is missing, namely a pro-social justice, anti-imperial perspective, which this writer shares, but which is only one of many possible perspectives (including the views of radical rightists or religious zealots).[54]

A more diverse media might have more so-called low-brow material than today, rather than less. Benjamin Compaine cites the chairman of the United States Federal Communications Commission complaining in 1961 of 'game shows, violence, audience participation shows, formula comedies ... blood and thunder, mayhem, violence, sadism, murder, western bad men, western good men, private eyes, gangsters ... and cartoons' in the media, and notes that in fact this seems to suggest a great deal of content diversity—just not the sort of content the chairman would have preferred.[55]

The idea that public broadcasting is needed to ensure the creation and distribution of 'quality' content has been a constant over the life of the ABC. It appears in the first discussions of public broadcasting in the United Kingdom, in the debates in 1932 in Australia, and is today used to justify the ABC's role in the digital world. In 2008 the ABC said it aimed to be a 'signpost for quality Australian content amidst limitless content choices', as its commercial rivals are increasingly compelled to produce 'tabloid content online'.[56] Advocates of ABC privatisation are frequently asked who, in the absence of the ABC, would produce quality content.[57] The term 'quality' is a value judgment as to what the private sector provides and the public demands. As the Austrian economist Ludwig von Mises explained, 'It is not the fault of the entrepreneurs that the consumers, the people, the common man, prefer liquor to Bibles and detective stories to serious books, and that governments prefer guns to butter'.[58] Quality is, of course, in the eye of the beholder.

But let us take this rationale at its face value, and accept for argument's sake that in fact public broadcasting exists as a subsidy to better quality content. In this argument, the market can only provide 'lowest common denominator' programming, which tends to be quickly and cheaply made game shows and reality television.[59] A public broadcaster, unconstrained by a need to maximise profits, is free to produce content that is more informative, more nuanced, more enriching and more experimental than private producers. It is certainly the case that game shows and reality television tend to be more prevalent on private broadcasters than public broadcasters.

Yet this casual observation is deeply misleading. The existence of the ABC has a dynamic effect on what is provided by the commercial broadcasters. In Chapter 4 we explore how the ABC has 'crowded-out' the provision of certain content by private providers, making it uneconomical for profit-maximising firms to produce the very quality material ABC defenders suggest would go unprovided. If private media outlets are producing only 'commercial trash', then that could very well be because the ABC has cornered the market for quality. Public broadcasting has existed in Australia almost as long as private broadcasting. Public and commercial television was introduced simultaneously. The idea that private broadcasters would not produce quality content was an assumption, not a discovery.

Indeed, a close reading of the early days of radio in Australia provides a much more ambiguous view of the provision of quality broadcasting. It is certainly the case that many supporters of public broadcasting saw the ABC as a subsidy to quality. Yet it was not the failures of the private B-class stations that they saw the ABC rectifying.

Throughout the 1932 debate the programming on the private B-class stations was often described as significantly higher quality than the semi-public licence-fee-supported A-class stations. Jack Beasley, then of Jack Lang's break-away Labor party, declared that he would 'not support those who condemn the part that is played by B class stations. It is my opinion that they are providing better programmes than those supplied by A class stations'.[60] The UAP member for Perth, Walter Nairn, declared that 'I wish to pay a tribute to the excellent work being done by B class stations. In Western Australia we are very much beholden to these stations for the programmes they put on the air, and I hope that more consideration will be given to them than they have had in the past'.[61] Thomas White, the member for the Victorian electorate of Balaclava, stated that 'the B class stations have given the best service'.[62] The Tasmanian Allan Guy connected this to the purpose of public broadcasting: 'We often hear of the merits of the methods of the British Broadcasting Corporation, but I venture to say that under our present system we obtain a programme just as good as that provided by the British Broadcasting Corporation'.

By contrast, the A-class stations were seen to be underperforming. Richard Casey, the UAP member for Corio in Victoria, summed up how many on both sides of politics saw the purpose of the new public broadcaster, as a way to force the A-class to improve their programming:

> While I have every reason to respect the B class stations in this country—and the energy and initiative of those controlling them, which is evidence of the strength and vigour

> of private enterprise in this country—I submit that the national broadcasting system must be the paramount entrepreneur of education and entertainment in Australia. Few will deny the scope for improvement in the present programmes issued from the A class stations. I do not mean that there is room for improvement only when these are judged by the highest cultural standards; there is room for improvement from the highest to the lightest of the items of entertainment.[63]

Even in the area of high-brow cultural content, members of parliament noted that the B-class stations were lacking. Frederick Stewart, the member for Parramatta, pointedly noted that 'only recently it was left to a B class station to put over the air the Australian Grand Opera chorus'. Indeed, the establishment of the Australian Broadcasting Company as the content producer for the A-class stations had been partly driven by dissatisfaction with the quality of programming. By contrast B-class stations prided themselves on delivering what the listeners wanted, and that philosophy reflected in their market share—the B-class stations commanded 80 per cent of the radio audience while the A-class stations commanded the remaining 20 per cent.[64]

There was and remains a deep cultural assumption that 'quality' media content aligns with what has, until recently, been described as 'high-brow' content—edifying classical music and long-form drama. Albert Green made the point explicitly when he contrasted the commercial broadcasters airing 'modern syncopated music, such as the "Kentucky Bunny Hug" or items like the "Two Black Crows"', and contrasting that with the need for the ABC to 'aim at a high standard'.[65]

The need for the provision of high quality content was an overriding preoccupation of the Royal Commission into Television. More than the introduction of radio, many special interest groups feared the coarsening effect of television, and the commission itself feared the 'mediocrity' of mass culture.

Our aim here is not to adjudicate a comparison between mass and elite culture. But commerce and culture are not opposed. As the economist Tyler Cowen demonstrates in his book *In Praise of Commercial Culture*, the market economy has in fact been a key mechanism for the development of high and low culture alike.[66] Market exchange caters for diverse cultural preferences, encourages the discovery and extension of tastes, and has sparked innovations that allow cultural producers and consumers to find, distribute and enjoy more and better cultural experiences. Cowen contrasts this view with the cultural pessimism that implies modernity and change have a corrupting influence on culture. It is no coincidence that when we think about the archetypal cultural content that might not be aired on commercial broadcasters we think of (for example) the plays of William Shakespeare (who wrote his first play in 1590) and classical music, rather than 'modern syncopated music'. But as Cowen writes, 'a culture already admired by the establishment usually is a culture whose best days lie in the past'.[67]

An even bolder defence of low-brow culture has been offered the University of Sydney cultural historian John Docker. Taking a distinctly left-libertarian perspective, Docker compares the much-maligned game shows and soap operas on television with earlier forms of cultural production and engagement that left-leaning historians and cultural theorists have lauded in early modern societies. Through this window, apparently disposable game shows look a lot like the European carnival games through which participants and audiences played with concepts of 'fortune and misfortune, gain and loss, crowning of temporary victors [and] uncrowning'.[68] Likewise the cheap soap opera looks like the literary melodramas of the nineteenth century, which, while disdained by the elite educated class, played a subversive and progressive role. Docker's contribution is to expose how that disdain has survived to inform concepts of the role of Australian broadcasting policy.

Paternalism

Paternalism describes an approach to public policy that uses the government to mould, change or reject the preferences of the citizens for their own good. Formally, paternalism refers to a situation where 'X acts to diminish Y's freedom, to the end that Y's good may be secured'.[69] Paternalistic policy can consist of the imposition of another's preferences about how they should act, or (as in the new philosophy of 'libertarian paternalism') an attempt to help individuals pursue their 'best' or most rational preferences.[70]

Media policy in Australia has always had a deeply paternalistic undercurrent. We can distinguish between two eras of public broadcasting paternalism in Australia. In the first, the paternalistic nature of the ABC was knowing and explicit. Paternalism formed a key part of the conception of public broadcasting from its first moments. In the second era, which extends to today, a paternalism undergirds the most common rationales for the continued existence of public broadcasting, albeit implicitly, discreetly, and—we suspect—for many advocates unconsciously.

The traditional idea of public broadcasting paternalism was

developed by John Reith. In his book *Broadcast over Britain*, published just a year after the BBC first went to air, Reith declared that 'it will be admitted by all that to have exploited so great a scientific invention for the purpose and pursuit of "entertainment" alone would have been a prostitution of its powers and an insult to the character and intelligence of the people'.[71] He went on, in a passage which clearly outlines his disdain for the preferences of the audience in the BBC's absence:

> Enjoyment may be sought, not with a view to returning refreshed to the day's work, but as a mere means of passing the time, and therefore of wasting it, or of relieving the tedium of life which is induced by deficiency, mental or physical. On the other hand, it may be part of a systematic and sustained endeavour to re-create, to build up knowledge, experience and character, perhaps even in the face of obstacles. Broadcasting enjoys the co-operation of the leaders of that section of the community whose duty and pleasure it is to give relaxation to the rest, but it is also aided by the discoverers of the intellectual forces which are moulding humanity, who are striving to show how time may be occupied not only agreeably, but well.[72]

This paternalism consisted of judgments about both the quality of content and the messages which that content sent the audience. For Reith, the 'preservation of a high moral standard is obviously of paramount importance'. The BBC would refrain from 'anything approaching vulgarity or directing attention to unsavoury subjects'. This, Reith noted, specifically excluded excessive discussion about horse racing or starting prices, as these 'might be the first inducement to systematic gambling'. The BBC must 'carry into the greatest possible number of homes everything that is best in every department of human knowledge, endeavour and achievement, and to avoid the things which are, or may be harmful'.[73] The broadcaster 'should come to be regarded, as I know with some he is, as guide, philosopher and friend'.[74] The Reithian philosophy of public broadcasting came to be identified with this paternalistic statement: 'few know what they want, and very few what they need'.[75]

Reith's ideas of public broadcasting were extremely influential in Australia. Even though the purity of his monopolistic paternalism was not adopted, the principles that guided it were. Australian legislators admired the BBC as 'such a convenient, flexible instrumentality for informing and moulding public opinion', in the words of Billy Hughes.[76] The ABC would be a 'supremely important agency for the moulding of the character of the people, the educating of public opinion, the elevation of the taste of the community, and the recreating of spiritual impulses'.[77] Victor Thompson, the Country Party member in New England, complained that 'The public of Australia has not been educated to appreciate high-class programmes. Various ballots taken by newspapers show that the most popular items are band music and gramophone records, which cannot be called high-class music'.[78]

Again the Royal Commission on Television is a rich source of disdain about the desires of mass audiences and the quality of popular media. In his evidence to the commission, the Secretary of the ACTU explicitly rejected the tastes and preferences of the working-class population that he represented, when he declared the principle that because 'it is popular, it does not necessarily mean that it is best for the community at large'.[79] The commission concluded that 'it is untrue to say that the public cannot be made to appreciate programmes of quality' and that television—both the ABC and the commercial broadcasters—should be controlled:

> in order to provide not only for the entertainment and enjoyment of viewers, but also for their education ... and enlightenment. The use of this new medium of communication must, in our view, be regarded, by commercial as well as national stations, as in the nature of a public trust for the benefit of all members of society.[80]

The Royal Commission on Television was the apogee of explicit public broadcasting paternalism. While the ABC continues to use the Reithian formulation of 'inform and entertain'—the phrase exists in the Charter—it does so with a distinctly different purpose: to rationalise its rejection of the market failure argument for public broadcasting. Nevertheless, there exists a strong line of paternalism in the arguments for the modern ABC. It comes to the fore when supporters of public broadcasting reckon with the fact that many of the 'problems' which public broadcasting is trying to solve have as their source the free choices of the audience—that audiences only want so much diversity, so much independence, and so much quality programming.

Take, for instance, the argument that public broadcasting is needed because of an apparent tendency of media audiences to seek out content that is congenial to them and that reinforces, rather than challenges, their biases. James Spigelman mounted the argument this way:

> One of the hidden dangers of the digital revolution is that it is now possible for citizens to retreat into an electronic vil-

> lage and insulate themselves from any opinion with which they might disagree. The threat of civic balkanisation is real.
>
> The role of public broadcasters: to promote social cohesion, nourish our national memory and identity, enrich our communal life and provide a forum for debate in a democratic polity as a whole, has become even more important.[81]

The core of this argument is known as balkanisation or cyber-balkanisation. The economist Cass Sunstein imagines a world in which media consumers prefer to consume ideologically narrow media.[82] It is questionable how much balkanisation is a reality for most media consumers, and the evidence seems to suggest that it only describes the most extreme partisan or ideological audiences.[83] Nevertheless, it is far from obvious what role public broadcasting can play in such an environment. The ABC is not a monopoly media content provider. To the extent that audiences are seeking ideologically uniform media content, a public broadcaster is not in a position to challenge those preferences. Rather, the predictions of further balkanisation seem to suggest that interest in a public broadcaster whose mission is pluralism and diversity will decline. A balkanising media environment spells doom for a public broadcaster.

Yet this concern neatly encapsulates the paternalism of modern public broadcasting, in that it sees public broadcasting as something 'done to' an audience rather than sought after. It is possible, and has always been possible, to identify market failures in the media that may make it harder for willing producers of content to supply willing consumers of content, as we have shown above. But it is also undeniable that market provision of media content is a reasonable reflection of the demands of the audience. Arguments for public broadcasting too often imply that diversity and pluralism, quality and independence are values which should be supplied to an audience that does not necessarily seek them.

As audiences fragment further—as the traditional broadcasting audience spills onto new digital platforms and new services—the implied paternalism of this approach is likely to get more and more discordant. A philosophy that maintains that audiences do not really know what they want is going to be harder and harder to sustain in a world where audiences can choose whatever they want from a near infinite range of sources.

Rural subsidy

At times the most basic rationale for the ABC's existence has been its role in providing regional, rural and remote broadcasting services. As James Fenton stated when introducing the ABC bill, 'Broadcasting would be a simple operation if it were merely to serve city interests, but, particularly in countries of wide expanses, the cities must contribute more or less to the privileges enjoyed by the rural folk'.[84] The Mansfield review argued that 'the ABC provides a "life-line", delivering much needed information and entertainment to the population of isolated regions'.[85] It is certainly true that marginally more rural and regional Australians watch ABC broadcasts than those living in capital cities. For example, in 2015-16, ABC News 24 had a weekly reach of 14.9 per cent of the metropolitan population, and an 18.9 per cent weekly reach of the regional population.[86] For its part, the ABC says it has 'a strong and unwavering commitment to rural and regional Australia'.[87]

Yet if rural subsidy is a central role for public broadcasting, it is peculiar that neither the ABC nor the government have sought to formally endorse it. The Mansfield review noted that 'the temptation will always exist for [ABC] management to cut in these areas because it could provoke a less audible outcry than cuts in areas where the strength and volume of opposition may be greater'.[88] The review recommended that a positive obligation to produce rural and regionally focused media be added to the Charter. Yet the only change to the Charter in the two decades since has been to authorise the ABC's digital offerings.

The response to a private members bill introduced by the Nationals Senator Bridget McKenzie in 2015 that proposes replacing 'cultural diversity' in the Charter with 'geographic and cultural diversity' is indicative of the ABC's attitude to its regional mandate.[89] The ABC argued that the Charter already requires it to support regional communities, which apparently it does so successfully. It argued that regional media was implied by the existing language which covering 'national identity' and 'cultural diversity'. And the ABC aggressively rejected any proposal to amend the Charter, suggesting that any clarification of the Charter would be a violation—possibly a political violation—of the ABC's independence:

> Operational and editorial independence are an important safeguard against political interference in the activities of the Corporation and ensure that funding priorities are made in the best interests of audiences and the community.
>
> Amending the Act and Charter is something that should be undertaken with considerable caution.[90]

In fact, the ABC has made some significant steps to reduce its regional offerings. Early in 2017 the ABC announced it would employ 80 new regional journalism jobs. Yet this comes after a long reduction in the emphasis and prominence given to regional journalism. In 2014 the ABC cancelled its state based and regionally focused flagship Stateline, first replacing it with a state based 7:30 program, only then to finally cancel that program in 2016. New national services—such as ABC News 24—have reportedly been financed at the expense of regional services.[91] Regional services also bore much of the brunt of the ABC's budget cut after the 2014 budget, as services and management continued to be centralised.[92]

Nevertheless, how desirable is it that public broadcasting is a subsidy to remote and regional Australia? Australia has significantly urbanised since the ABC was founded. In 1932, 36 per cent of Australians lived in rural areas. Today that figure has declined to just 10.8 per cent.[93] The ABC budget has increased significantly in this time. The University of Melbourne economist John Freebairn has examined the arguments for regional subsidies and region-specific policies. While he did not consider the case of broadcasting, the principles he outlines can easily be applied to the ABC. Freebairn argues that 'society's equity concerns are best addressed by instruments which focus on the circumstances of individuals and households, rather than on industries and regions'.[94] Policies based on individual and house characteristics are going to be more efficient than those based on location or region. Government services should be equitably supplied. The regional analyst Paul Collits points out that the guiding principles to apply to regional policy should be subsidiarity—that is, local regions should make decisions for themselves, rather than have their services controlled from a distance.[95]

It is also important to point out that while regional media

is certainly in flux there has been no better time for people in regional and remote areas to access and produce content. The limiting principle for media access is no longer the signals of individual broadcasters but internet access and speed. To the extent that this barrier has been overcome—and it is certainly the case that supplying high speed internet is more costly in remote areas than capital cities—regional consumers have exactly the same media access as those who live in the most densely populated areas of the country.

The ability to produce local content has also never been stronger. Regional communities are like any other community: when they have common interests producers will seek to service those interests. The sharp decline in media production and distribution through digital technology opens up vast new opportunities for local content, even as traditional vehicles are shrinking or shutting their doors. Collits warns against 'declinism' in discussions about regional policy.[96] Nowhere is this more obvious than in discussions of regional media. While the ABC exists it should service urban and regional communities equitably. There is no distinct case for public broadcasting as a rural subsidy.

Australian content

The idea that public broadcasting has a special responsibility to create and distribute Australian content is deep within the conception of the ABC. Where the Charter is vague and unclear on almost all aspects of what the ABC should do, it is unambiguous on Australian content. The ABC has to 'contribute to a sense of national identity' and 'reflect the cultural diversity of the Australian community'. This is enhanced by its requirement to broadcast outside of Australia content which 'encourages awareness of Australia and an international understanding of Australian attitudes on world affairs', as well as broadcast 'information about Australian affairs and Australian attitudes on world affairs' to Australians living abroad.

But the ABC is only one of the vast network of policies intended to boost the creation and distribution of Australian content. The Gillard government's banner national cultural policy, Creative Australia, identified dozens of Commonwealth programs and initiatives that aim in large part to subsidise and support Australian cultural production, distribution and training.[97] These include Screen Australia, the Australia Council, Creative Partnerships, the Australian Film, Television and Radio School, the National Film and Sound Archive of Australia, as well as museums such as the Australian National Maritime Museum, National Gallery of Australia, National Library of Australia, National Museum of Australia and the Museum of Australian Democracy. The Commonwealth also supports training bodies such as the Australian Youth Orchestra, Australian Ballet School, Australian National Academy of Music, the Flying Fruit Fly Circus, the National Aboriginal and Islander Skills Development Association Dance College, the National Institute of Circus Arts, and the National Institute of Dramatic Art.

On top of these formal organisations, the Commonwealth supports regional cultural infrastructure, touring programs and festivals, indigenous cultural programs and employment, art financing and leasing programs, programs to attract foreign productions to Australian locations (thereby increasing the Australian content of foreign films), literary programs, and the Enterprise Connect Creative Industries Innovation Centre.

In addition to all of this, every state and territory also has its own cultural programs, subsidies, museums, and other various initiatives that aim to boost the production and distribution of Australian content to more than what a free market would apparently supply. Cultural production is also subsidised through the tax and regulatory system. The Commonwealth offers taxation offsets for cultural gifts and organisations, and the Australian Screen Production Incentive supports film-making through the tax system. Commercial radio and television broadcasters are subject to minimum Australian content requirements. Subscription television services are required to spend a minimum amount on the production of Australian drama.

Even this understates the volume of government intervention in the cultural market. As Tyler Cowen notes in his appraisal of American cultural policy, a subsidies to educational institutions, research and innovation programs, and as tax breaks for religious bodies and non-profit organisations subsidise cultural production.[98] Public service jobs in unrelated, non-cultural fields can be considered as 'support' for the arts. The light workload of the bureaucracy allows public servants to produce culture on the side. Finally, the vast regime of intellectual property is a 'subsidy' to cultural production, insofar as its stated policy goal is to increase the supply of cultural production to more than would be supplied in a free market.[99]

As this shows, public broadcasting is only one component of government intervention into the supply and demand of Australian culture. And it is unlikely to be the most efficient. The ABC commissions, produces and distributes content through its broadcasting network. The policy necessity of each of these tasks depends on how we formulate the 'problem' that subsidies to Australian content are trying to solve.

Is the problem that a market will fail to produce the level of Australian content that the audience desires? A 2011 report by Screen Australia found that Australian content was being crowded out of the marketplace by cheaper foreign—particularly American—content.[100] It is cheaper to purchase the rights to an American production than an Australian one, partly because of the high costs of producing in Australia and partly because the larger American markets allow for more efficient and profitable production. This was described by Screen Australia in the press as the equivalent of 'dumping', where goods are exported to be sold at prices below domestic goods prices in that foreign market.[101] But if this argument is correct, the ABC's role—or, indeed, any intervention into the cultural market—should be limited to subsidising content creation. Once Australian content is as affordable as equivalent foreign content, consumers will be free to follow their preferences.

An alternative explanation for the existence of the ABC's role in commissioning and distributing Australian media is a paternalistic one: audiences might either not know how good Australian media is, or may need to be nudged into consuming it.[102] The ABC is valuable in this conception because it guarantees that Australian content is broadcast—pushed—to every citizen. At its most benign this could be described as a version of an economic information problem: audiences do not necessarily know about the cultural content available to them. If so, then a cheaper and less burdensome solution would be to tackle the problem directly and have the government sponsor public advertisements for Australian content. Public broadcasting is a very expensive, and rather indirect, way to inform people about the quality of Australian content.

A less benign interpretation is that Australian content policy is designed to push Australian content to audiences with the goal of influencing their tastes and preferences. This cynical claim is reinforced by the Charter itself, which directs the statutory corporation to 'contribute to a sense of national identity'. Through its public broadcaster, the government seeks to create an identity for Australians that goes beyond the liberal belief in adherence to a set of values (such as tolerance, the rule of law, and equality). While it is beyond doubt that government intervention can change tastes and preferences—all tastes and preferences are socially informed through a process of experimentation and discovery—it is not at all clear why we should welcome a democratic government that seeks to manipulate its citizens in this way.[103]

Democracy

For a nation to be considered democratic, it requires economic and political institutions that allow for its government to be freely scrutinised and criticised. The American founder Thomas Jefferson put the sentiment this way: 'The only security of all is in a free press. The force of public opinion cannot be resisted when permitted freely to be expressed. The agitation it produces must be submitted to. It is necessary, to keep the waters pure.'[104] Democratic theorists have endorsed Jefferson's view, considering freedom of speech and freedom of the press to be an essential ingredient in democratic governance.[105] The High Court of Australia has also followed this line of argument, 'discovering' in the Australian Constitution an implied right to political communication on the grounds of the country's democratic structure.[106]

These assertions of the importance of a free press, however, do not necessarily imply that the government should subsidise the press. To the contrary, many non-democratic nations have maintained very high levels of government ownership and subsidy in the media. We have already cast some doubts on the argument that democracies require public broadcasters. While the ABC is proud of its apparent independence of the government of the day it remains entirely reliant on the government's budget and is regularly asked to account for its editorial choices by elected politicians. Looking at public broadcasters around the world, Andrei Shleifer and his colleagues found that government-funded broadcasting is associated with less liberal, less democratic regimes.[107]

It has often been claimed by the ABC that technological change means public broadcasting has a more important role to play than ever. In his final speech as ABC managing director, Mark Scott outlined in detail the effect that technology and audience fragmentation had had on Australia's incumbent media providers, including the closure of newspapers and shrinking of workforces. He concluded that 'A well-funded ABC is one sure bet in an uncertain, unstable media world'.[108] Yet public broadcasting can have a distorting effect on the democratic market for ideas. Government interventions typically have consequences, intended or unintended, that go beyond their original policy rationale. Chapter 4 explores the burdens of the ABC. In particular, the ABC systematically favours one side of politics, and has a crowding-out effect on commercial broadcasters. These characteristics undermine the claims that public broadcasting has a central supporting role for democracy: in practice the ABC is partial, has a distorting effect on political life, and undermines commercial broadcasters. The next chapter contains a detailed elaboration of these arguments.

That is not to deny that the media market is not going through major changes that could have material consequences for journalism and public scrutiny of government. But the problem faced by commercial news organisations is too much online competition—too much news, too much opinion, too many outlets, too much fragmentation, and too much disaggregation. The policy response to the problem of media scarcity in the 1930s was public broadcasting. It would be surprising if the policy response to the problem of media abundance in the 2010s was also public broadcasting.

We do not propose to solve the problem faced by private media organisations here. Market development is experimental and evolutionary. Observing the rich and vibrant media market in the United States—especially that focused on investigative journalism and politics—should give much reason for optimism. Digital technologies have encouraged large numbers of new entrants, covering niche and mainstream audiences, and revitalised existing media conglomerates. The dire situation of Fairfax newspapers in Australia should be contrasted with the thriving *Washington Post* and *New York Times*, both left-of-centre newspapers that have made better business decisions than the *Age* and the *Sydney Morning Herald*. The news media industry is an entrepreneurial ecosystem, and while we are sure that it will adapt to technological change, that adaptation will be quicker, and more consumer-focused, if government intervention in the form of regulation and public broadcasting is kept to a minimum.

Nevertheless, there are positive approaches the government could take to the changes in the media landscape. A general protection of freedom of speech might be seen as an 'intervention' in the media market in the interests of democracy. A positive response to the turmoil in the media would be to reduce limitations to freedom of speech. From a democratic perspective, more attention should be paid to the chilling effect of limits on speech than to changes in the market structure for journalism.

Other arguments

There have been other arguments mounted for public broadcasting that resist the sort of analysis offered here. Historically, one of the significant justifications for the ABC has been a generalised fear of technology. In this argument, broadcasting is just too important not to be controlled by the government. As one parliamentarian stated in 1948 during debate about the introduction of television licences, 'Broadcasting is already the most important means of entertainment and expression in this country. With the coming of television and facsimile, its power and importance will grow greatly'.[109] Another argued in 1932 that

> Many persons who are not Labour sympathizers, believe that broadcasting is a matter which lends itself peculiarly to some system of national control. It is a great utility, and an important form of entertainment, which enters into the lives of the most remote dwellers in the backblocks, and for that reason should not be made a means of private profit. Our Government, therefore, decided to institute a system of national control.[110]

This argument, that the government should be involved in broadcasting just because it is an important technology, is anachronistic. The ABC acquired radio and television broadcasting at a moment in Australian history when public ownership was in its ascendancy; the decades since their introduction have seen a reduction in direct government ownership of industry and a reliance on regulation as a means of social control. It is doubly anachronistic because new technology has eroded the pre-eminence of broadcasting. In an age of technological convergence it is hard to argue that broadcasting stands above other media forms. But more fundamentally, these arguments reveal a fear of technology which has shown to be unwarranted—broadcasting has not undermined critical thought, as so many witnesses to the 1954 Royal Commission on Television feared it would.[111]

Less anachronistic, but similarly hard to counter, is the aesthetic argument for public broadcasting. The occasional proposals to allow the ABC to take advertising—thereby giving it a surer financial foundation—have been rejected not only for fear that doing so would undermine the ABC's 'independence' but as an aesthetic dislike of advertising in general. This too has a long history. The United Australia Party's Eric Harrison complained during the 1932 debate that the need for commercial stations to fund their operations were ruining the enjoyment of their programmes:

> The A class stations should cater for the aesthetic and educational requirements of the public. The average listener, after hearing a fine piece of music from an A class station, is not prepared to listen to a programme, the real object of which is to bring before the public the merits

> of Blogg's pills. He prefers to meditate on the music he has heard.[112]

Broadcasting, of course, has to be funded, and advertising has its virtues: rather than having audiences finance the content, private companies provide the content to consumers for free. Subscription television funds itself through a mixture of advertising and subscription, and online media organisations are experimenting with various combinations of these financial streams and new approaches. No doubt aesthetic objections to advertising are real. But aesthetic objections to advertising are not enough to rationalise the construction of a billion-dollar public policy initiative that is consumed by a fraction of the Australian population. In the next chapter we examine the costs, and consequences, of this expenditure.

4 The burden of the ABC

In this chapter we outline the many burdens associated with the ABC—its fiscal cost as well as the effect it has on the Australian media and political culture. These burdens should not be seen as a bug, but rather a feature of Australian public broadcasting—they exist by design, not accident. Here we consider the ABC through three prisms: as a bureaucracy, as a non-profit firm, and as a political actor. All three perspectives allow us to clarify the relationship between the ABC's structure and its burden.

The ABC as a bureaucracy

First and foremost the ABC is a bureaucracy. The ABC meets the economist William Niskanen's definition of a bureau: 'Bureaus are non-profit organisations that are financed, in part, from a periodic appropriation or grant.'[1] The financing of the organisation is important—some government organisations are financed through the sale of goods or services. Those government agencies or utilities are not bureaucracies per se under this definition. The ABC, however, is a bureaucracy even though its employees are not employed under the Public Service Act.

Niskanen differentiates two traditions of thought about bureaucracy—an intellectual tradition and a populist tradition. The intellectual tradition says that a bureaucratic structure allows good people to do good work without being subject to the whim of the market. The ABC as an organisation certainly propagates the view that it operates under this tradition. The populist tradition of bureaucracy is less complimentary to bureaucrats—as Niskanen suggests, here bureaucracies are seen as being 'inefficient, oversized, and oppressive'. Bureaucrats are 'dumb, lazy, malevolent, and/or venal'.[2] Both characterisations are somewhat unfair and inappropriate. As Gordon Tullock—one of the founders of the public choice school of economics—has explained:

> Bureaucrats are much like other people and, like people in general, are more interested in their own well-being than in the public interest. The problem is to design an apparatus that leads bureaucrats in their own interest to serve the interests of the rest of us.[3]

Of course, in the ABC's context there is no mechanism to ensure that the ABC serves the interests of those who pay for it. The general point, however, remains the same. People can be expected to pursue their own self-interest unless otherwise incentivised. ABC employees are no different. To the extent that the ABC is a bureaucracy, the ABC can be expected to behave accordingly. Niskanen argues that bureaucracies seek to maximise their discretionary budget, while Gordon Tullock argues that they act to maximise the size of the organisation. These alternate theories are not mutually exclusive—in each instance the bureaucrats maximise budget or size for much the same reasons. In each instance this allows bureaucratic management to gain power, prestige, larger salaries, patronage, and better working conditions.

It is indicative of the ABC's self-interest in this area that one of its most famous publicity campaigns directly addressed the fiscal burden of public broadcasting. The 'eight cents a day' slogan formed part of an aggressive campaign waged by the ABC's then chairman David Hill for more government support in 1987 and 1988. As the ABC's budget at the time was around $430 million a year and the Australian population around 17 million the figure of eight cents was, Ken Inglis writes, 'pretty accurate'.[4] A similar calculation shows that the ABC now costs each Australian about 14 cents per day. In an analysis showing a willingness-to-pay comparison between the ABC and the subscription television service Foxtel, QUT academics Brian McNair and Adam Swift asked this question:

> But who can seriously maintain, given around 2.5 million Australians pay nearly hundreds of dollars a year to Foxtel, that 14 cents a day for the ABC's content is excessive?[5]

When stated in those terms it seems almost churlish to resent being deprived of 14 cents per day to pay for the ABC. It isn't clear, however, why a per capita calculation is appropriate. Taxpayers finance the ABC, so the more appropriate calculation might be per taxpayer—an adjustment which would see the 14 cents per day doubled. We could go further and argue that only those taxpayers who pay more tax than they receive in social welfare payments pay for the ABC. Nevertheless the figure would no doubt remain substantially lower than the few dollars per day that subscribers pay for Foxtel.

Yet this question itself is not the most obvious question to ask. The 14 cents per day is not a voluntary transaction but is taken from citizens through taxation and threats of imprisonment for non-payment. Surely a far more interesting question to ask—and perhaps answer—is why do millions of Australians choose to pay hundreds of dollars per year to watch subscription television when the ABC provides those services—and apparently more—for a mere 14 cents per day? A further point to raise is that government policy should not be evaluated on how cheap (or expensive, for that matter) it is but rather on how effective it is, and how otherwise that funding could be deployed or how else those policy objectives could be achieved.

Figure 1 shows ABC funding since 1970-71 to the present in 2015/16 dollars.[6] The $55.4 million allocated to the ABC in 1970-71 equates to some $598.5 million in 2016 dollars.[7] In other words, at a time when media choice and opportunity have massively increased, so too the ABC has grown.

Yet we are invited to believe all that growth is good value. McNair and Swift point our attention to the ABC Annual Reports that usually contain survey data demonstrating how Australians perceive the ABC. The ABC's satisfaction indicators are very impressive. A selection of those indicators

Figure 1: Government funding for the Australian Broadcasting Commission / Corporation, 1970-71—2015-16

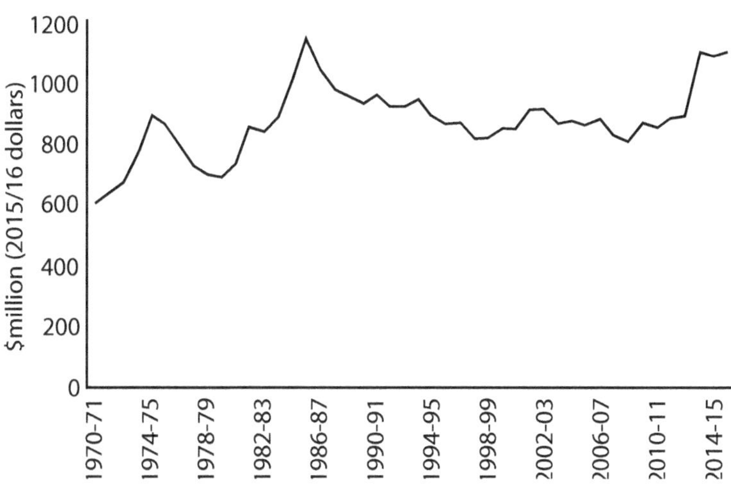

(Excludes funding for transmission costs and capital use charges. Data include equity injections and orchestral subsidies.)

are shown in Table 1. Eighty-six per cent of Australians value the ABC. Seventy-seven per cent think it is balanced and even-handed. Seventy-eight per cent think ABC television provides quality programming.

This rosy picture is complicated by the fact that ABC television only had a 17.6 per cent share of the primetime five-city metro market in 2015-16. Indeed, there is a huge gap between the number of people who claim to value the ABC, and those people who actually consume its services. It is also noteworthy that more people in the metro areas consume ABC radio than primetime television and the percentage of people who believe that the ABC provides quality radio

Table 1: Selected satisfaction indicators and actual ABC audiences

	2016	2015	2014	2013
Selected Satisfaction Indicators				
Percentage of people who believe the ABC provides quality programming				
Television	78	78	78	78
Radio	63	62	61	64
Percentage of people who believe the ABC is balanced and even-handed when reporting news and current affairs	77	77	77	78
Percentage of people who value the ABC and its services to the community	86	84	84	85
Percentage of people who believe the ABC is efficient and well managed	69	69	68	69
Actual Audience				
Television: Daytime Share 5-city Metro	26.2	27.4	26.5	24.3
Television: Primetime Share 5-city Metro	17.6	17.7	18.1	17.8
Television: Daytime Share Regional	30.1	31.6	29.7	27.9
Television: Primetime Share Regional	19.4	19.2	20.1	19.5
Radio: 5 City Metro	23.9	23.7	24.1	24.2

Source: ABC Annual Reports (various)

programming is much lower (63 per cent) than those who believe the ABC provides quality television programming (78 per cent). It appears that the more people know about the ABC the less they value it.

This kind of result is not necessarily surprising—it is very likely that Australians have been socialised into believing that the ABC provides a quality service as opposed to having actually experienced that quality through their own viewing or listening.

It is true that the ABC has higher market share in regional areas than it does in metropolitan areas—yet even there the gap between what people say about the ABC and their actual consumption of ABC services is large. Unfortunately the ABC does not appear to publish market share data for its regional radio services. It is one thing to be assured by politicians that the ABC provides valuable services to the community but it would be even more reassuring to see the actual data supporting that claim.

What we do know, however, is that the ABC is a large well-funded government entity that assures the Australian population that it is doing a good job, that the Australian population largely believe is doing a good job, yet ABC services are actually consumed by only a very small number of Australians.

The ABC as a non-profit firm

Economists routinely assume that firms attempt to maximise profit—much of modern economics builds on that assumption. But in the mid to late twentieth century economists had two important—but related—insights. First, organisations may not always act in their owners' best interests. This is now widely discussed as the principal-agent problem or the separation of ownership and control. The second insight was to model how organisations might behave if they did not maximise profit. The great economist Armen Alchian emphasised that these so-called managerial theories worked best when applied to (highly) regulated firms or those under government ownership.[8]

The ABC very clearly is separated from control from its ultimate owners—the citizens of Australia (at least if we adopt a romantic ideal of state-owned enterprises). Citizens exercise limited and indirect control over the parliament. The parliament in turn exercises limited control over the executive that in turn has formally divorced itself from any meaningful control over the ABC. True—the government of the day appoints the ABC Board, but since 2007 only from a short-list prepared by a nomination panel. The Board then selects a managing director who has responsibility for the day-to-day management of the ABC. There is no accountability mechanism that links the managing director to the citizens. If the ultimate owners dislike what they see and/or hear on the ABC the only governance mechanism available to them is the equivalent of the Wall Street walk—that is, switch off or change channels. They still, however, have to stump up their 14 cents per day.

There is a second level of separation. The ABC Charter sets out the ABC's objectives—presumably what it is Australians want from the ABC. Yet the Charter has no enforcement mechanism. Very clearly there is a strong and well defined separation between the ownership and control of the ABC. Of course, it can be argued that this is by design; to ensure the independence of the ABC. But that policy choice and design is very likely to have consequences. These managerial theories suggest firms will act in certain ways. William Baumol, for example, suggested that managers may attempt to maximise sales. In the case of the ABC this could be interpreted as maximising output. Robin Marris suggested the firm will seek to maximise its growth, while Oliver Williamson—the 2009 Nobel economics laureate—argued that managers would maximise their own utility through emoluments, staff expenditure, and discretionary investment.[9] Armen Alchian concludes that Williamson's model is the most powerful of the three—he is dismissive of concepts such as 'satisficing' (that is, doing the bare minimum) arguing that it is more of a constraint than an objective. In combination these theories suggest that the ABC will expand to beyond its profit-maximising size, will expand into more markets than it otherwise should, and that the ABC will pursue its own objectives rather than those set out in its Charter. In practice that last point means that the ABC (and individual employees) will interpret the ABC Charter opportunistically, allowing them to pursue their own agendas.

An immediate criticism of this analysis would be to argue that the ABC makes no profit, so how then can we talk about a profit-maximising size? Not making a profit is a policy choice, not a market outcome. The ABC chooses to expand its operations and incur costs to exhaust the funds available for expenditure. It can continue to operate at levels of output where its commercial competitors would be unprofitable. This potential crowding-out effect could and arguably does distort the market. Greg Hywood, the Fairfax CEO, told the Select Committee on the Future of Public Interest Journalism in May 2017:

> The Australian Broadcasting Corporation is creating additional pressure on local commercial media by aggressively competing for the same audience that commercial media rely on and providing online content for free, undermining our ability to create a sustainable model. The ABC also, out of taxpayers' money, pays Google, who pay negligible tax and

> spend nothing on local content provision, for search engine marketing. That means that the ABC stories appear higher on key search terms such as national news, international news et cetera, and restricts our ability to generate revenue from our audience.
>
> We believe that the biggest threat to quality journalism in this country is unprofitable local media companies.[10]

Hywood's argument, however, has not gone unchallenged. Writing in *The Conversation*, QUT professor Axel Bruns argued that the *Sydney Morning Herald* website in fact 'consistently attracts a much larger volume of visits than *ABC News*', and only slightly more than the *Age*, and all are roundly beaten by *news.com.au*. Bruns concluded that 'if the ABC is undermining Fairfax's market position, it's not making a very good job of it'.[11]

In the very first instance this argument suggests that the ABC is underperforming. Fairfax Media has a market capitalisation of just under three billion dollars while the ABC has an operating budget of over one billion dollars, yet Fairfax—an organisation widely perceived as being in decline—has twice as many visits than the ABC on just two of its news websites. Nevertheless, it is not clear that Bruns is comparing like with like. He compares *ABC News* to the Fairfax newspapers—but newspapers do not only report news, they also provide lifestyle, travel and other 'soft' stories. *ABC News* may have fewer visits than the Fairfax newspapers, but the entirety of the ABC might not. Bruns, however, goes further, arguing that the ABC drives traffic to Fairfax but that Fairfax does not direct traffic its competitors, given that the public broadcaster 'has long partnered with Microsoft's Bing search engine to include a block of links to related content from elsewhere on the web alongside its own stories'. Yet Bruns admits that 'The *SMH* receives the vast plurality of its inbound reader traffic from Google sites'. So Hywood's argument that the ABC pays Google for search engine marketing is not entirely countered by Bruns' argument about Bing. Nonetheless Bruns' overall position is quite correct:

> The traffic patterns we have seen here, at any rate, reveal that audiences lost to *ABC News* should be the least of Greg Hywood's worries. The major Fairfax sites consistently outperform the ABC in terms of reader traffic, and the public broadcaster is even a net source of visits to the *SMH* and *The Age*.

Fairfax Media also owns radio stations that compete directly with ABC radio stations and outperform the ABC in market share. Again it appears that despite its massive funding advantage over commercial operations the ABC underperforms with audiences. Hywood's argument is that the ABC cannibalises the market while Bruns argues the ABC grows the market. The evidence does not strongly favour Hywood's position—to the extent that the Fairfax radio stations perform well while the newspapers do not, it is more likely the newspapers have poor market position or editorial policies.

There is a stronger case to be made that the ABC has crowded out the private media market in television shows. For example, the creation of the ABC Kids television channels led to a sharp decline in viewership of the children's television programming being provided by the commercial networks. This was despite regulatory controls administered by the government that required commercial networks to air a minimum amount of children's programming. The Australian reported that the ABC's moves led to a significant reduction in the private sector broadcasters' investment in children's programming.[12] There is no evidence to suggest the commercial market was under-performing before the creation of the ABC children's channels, and the commercial networks were compliant with local content rules. The ABC, however, expanded into the market and is not bound by the local content rule that binds commercial providers. It appears that children and/or their parents prefer commercial-free television while enjoying the better international children's television shows that the local commercial providers cannot always show. Unravelling the net effects of the several market distortions would be a complex task—the local content rule, the asymmetric application of that rule, the preference for international shows over local shows, the lack of advertising and so on all feed into a situation where the public broadcaster has crowded out local commercial broadcasters.

A similar example of the ABC crowding out private sector media efforts is fact-checking outlets. In recent years a number of news organisations have established dedicated fact-checking units.[13] Fact-checking websites were intended as a rejection of the 'he-said, she-said' style of journalism that simply reported rather than scrutinised the statements of public figures. Pioneered in the United States, a number of private fact-checking services began in Australia in 2012 and 2013. *Politifact Australia*, an offshoot of the American firm of the same name, was established by the former *Sydney Morning Herald* editor Peter Fray. Fairfax Media also established its own fact-checking program. However, plans for developing these services were cut short by the $10 million granted to the ABC at the end of the Gillard government in part to support the establishment of an ABC fact-checking service. Announcing a reduction from seven full-time staff to three part-time staff, Fray told the press that 'We don't have the budget the ABC does and taxpayers' funding'.[14] *Politifact Australia* has since closed.

A final area where we are likely to observe some crowding out is in the labour market. The reason ABC employees are not employed under the Public Service Act is because the ABC wants to be able to offer terms and conditions that allow it to compete with the commercial sector for talent. At the same time, however, it appears that ABC working conditions approximate those in the public sector (that tend to be less well remunerated). For example, the paid maternity leave provisions at the ABC used to leverage off the Maternity Leave (Commonwealth Employees) Act 1973. Commercial media compete to sell advertising to audiences. Those media personalities who are best able to attract large advertising audiences get paid more than those who do not. The ABC, however, does not advertise. So what is the basis by which we can determine the value of any particular ABC employee? One basis might well be audience size. But there is no relationship between audience size and revenue to the ABC, and the ABC does not believe that maximising its audience is its only mission. There is also no obvious relationship between exposure and income at the ABC.

In 2013 ABC salary data was leaked to the Australian newspaper.[15] This data revealed that the ABC pays more than $250,000 to eight different broadcasters. The highest salaried broadcaster was Tony Jones, who received $350,000. The data also showed that of the ABC's then $1.03 billion annual budget, $465 million was spent on wages, superannuation and other entitlements. In the 2012-13 financial year the ABC had 4664 full-time-equivalent employees. That implies an employee cost (wages, superannuation and other entitlements) of $99,670 per employee. Unsurprisingly some ABC employees earn more than others. But what is surprising is that *Q&A* host Tony Jones earned $350,000 in that year. *Q&A* is a one-hour show per week that runs for nine to ten months of the year. Leigh Sales, the host of the weekday *7.30 Report*, earned much less on $280,400. That gap, however, cannot easily be explained by gender discrimination. The NSW newsreader Juanita Phillips earned $316,454 while her Victorian counterpart Ian Henderson earned a mere $188,533. Jon Faine, ABC Melbourne morning host, 'cheerfully confirm[ed]' that his salary, reported as $285,249, had recently been increased to $300,000.[16] In the absence of a market signal of value these salaries are hard to justify.

The ABC as a political actor

Journalism is an intellectual profession. Most journalists are engaged in 'communication with the public on intellectual themes by means of books, magazine articles, op-ed pieces, open letters, public lectures, and appearances on radio or television'.[17] Not every single employee of the ABC can be characterised as having an intellectual occupation under this definition—but at its core the primary focus of the ABC is intellectual. It exists to inform and educate, in that order.

There is good reason to suspect that intellectuals are more likely than not to have a left-wing orientation. Both Joseph Schumpeter and Friedrich von Hayek provide a theory of intellectuals. Joseph Schumpeter defined intellectuals as being people who 'wield the power of the spoken and the written word' but in 'the absence of direct responsibility for practical affairs'.[18] People with all care and no responsibility. Schumpeter provides a theory of incentives. Intellectuals are forever questioning—and attacking—social institutions. By contrast, Hayek provides a psychological argument—intellectuals are rationalist and require detailed explanations of all phenomena.[19] This is a justification for that pejorative dismissal of intellectuals: 'that's all very well in practice, but it could never work in theory'. Hayek makes the prediction that the more intelligent an educated person is the more likely they are to hold socialist views. Particularly he suggests that highly intelligent left-wingers are more likely to choose an intellectual career path, while highly intelligent right-wingers are likely to choose another career path. To that extent, we are likely to see more people with left-wing views self-selecting into careers such as journalism.

This sort of argument is consistent with the journalist David Marr's 2004 observation, 'The natural culture of journalism is a kind of vaguely soft-left inquiry, sceptical of authority. I mean, that's just the world out of which journalists come. If they don't come out of this world, they really can't be reporters. I mean, if you are not sceptical of authority—find another job.'[20] The problem with Marr's observation, however, is that there might be more than just 'soft-left inquiry' going on. A 2013 survey of journalists revealed a large left-wing bias amongst ABC journalists compared to their colleagues at Fairfax and News. The bias was even more marked when compared to the general population.[21] In a survey of over 600 journalists the journalism academic Folker Hanusch asked journalists as to their political beliefs and voting intentions at the 2013 federal election. Table 2 summarises his results together with the actual voting results of the 2013 federal election.

Table 2: Journalists' voting intention at the 2013 federal election

	Greens	Labor	Coalition
ABC	41.2	32.4	14.7
Fairfax	19.8	54.7	19.8
News Limited	19.8	46.5	26.7
All Journalists	19.4	43.0	30.2
Senior Media Executives	11.4	34.1	43.2
Electorate at 2013 election (HR)	8.7	33.4	45.6
Electorate at 2013 election (Senate)	8.7	30.1	37.7

Source: Hanusch (2013), Australian Electoral Commission

Consistent with Marr's observation, journalists are more likely to be soft-left (defined as being a Labor voter) than the general population and less likely to be a Coalition voter. Journalists in general are about twice as likely to be Greens voters as the general population. Consider, however, the ABC—their journalists are nearly five times more likely to vote Greens than are the general population and twice as likely to be Greens voters than are journalists in general.

Of course, that does not mean that media consumers are destined to experience left-wing media—after all, there are right-wing media outlets. Hanusch, for example, reports that senior managers within media organisations are more likely to be Coalition supporters than Labor supporters. People also respond to incentives—some incentives push people to left-wing views (as Schumpeter suggested) while others push people to satisfying market niches where consumers may have either left-wing or right-wing views. As Richard Swedberg says in his introduction to Schumpeter's *Capitalism, Socialism and Democracy*, 'most intellectuals appear fairly well integrated into the various institutions in which they work'.[22] In short, individuals driving a personal agenda within an organisation represent an organisational failure. Fairfax would be an example of such an organisation—the so-called Charter of Editorial Independence at Fairfax operates to prevent senior management—including the board of directors—from effectively controlling the organisation.

Former ABC political editor Chris Uhlmann has acknowledged that the ABC has a perceived bias but counters that journalistic professionalism drives its media content above all:

> I had some bracing character assessments in more than a dozen conversations about my failings and the shortcomings of the ABC.
>
> According to them I, and the rest of my colleagues, are captured by the Left and don't even attempt to understand the grievances of that kind of crowd. They believe that we dismiss them as aging nutters, unworthy of our attention, except when we want to sketch a caricature. They believed that we would not report the event, or that we would ridicule it.
>
> Those kinds of sentiments are almost impossible to turn. To my eyes and ears the reports we filed were fair and I have always believed that I work with some of the finest

> journalists in Australia. But it would not surprise me if attendees watched our work that night and had all their fears confirmed.[23]

No doubt professional pride in the craft of journalism drives the content decisions of most ABC journalists, most of the time. But political bias need not be intentional. There is a long tradition in academic media and communications theory that focuses on uncovering hidden biases in media, focusing on the mechanisms by which that bias is manifest. Media effects theory says that what the media chooses to print or broadcast has consequences: a concrete and discernible impact on the society which consumes that media. For our purposes here, this academic study has focused on two mechanisms whereby that might occur. The first mechanism is the ability of the media to set the agenda of public debate.[24] Editors and producers have to make choices about what news to feature and how prominently. The front page of a newspaper frequently sets the political topics of the day, and what public policy issues that newspaper considers to be important are made important by their choice to focus on them. The second mechanism is the ability of media organisations—and individual journalists—to 'frame' their discussion about any given issue in a larger narrative.[25] For example, a story on renewable energy requirements that is preceded by a discussion on global climate change will be read by the audience very differently to one which is preceded by a discussion about high energy prices.

These agenda setting and framing decisions are not necessarily deliberate attempts to slant stories or manipulate audiences. But what journalists, producers and editors think is interesting will be displayed in their output. Media effects theory has long been used to criticise private sector media organisations.[26] In their book *Manufacturing Consent*, Noam Chomsky and Edward Herman famously described much private media as 'propaganda' in the service of the capitalism. Given the remarkably unrepresentative political views within the ABC uncovered by Folker Hanusch, the burden of proof is surely on those who believe that agenda setting and media framing theory does not apply to public broadcasters.

Direct and uncontested evidence for bias in the ABC is hard to come by. Bias, it is often said, is in the eye of the beholder. We have both seen our appearances on ABC programs used as evidence by some commentators—and many on social media—that the ABC is incorrigibly and unforgivably right wing. When this book was announced, ABC supporters immediately released a petition on Change.org to 'STOP [Institute of Public Affairs] "Operatives" from being on ABC MEDIA whilst they push for PRIVATISING AUNTY', declaring that 'On one hand they are WANTING TO SELL OFF AUNTY whilst on the other USING AUNTY TO SELL THEIR WARES. SICKOS!'[27]

There is a large academic literature that attempts to empirically establish whether the media is biased or not. For our purposes the important paper is by Tim Groseclose and Jeffrey Milyo published in the prestigious *Quarterly Journal of Economics* in 2005.[28] They provide an 'objective' measure of bias—or 'slant'—by comparing the number of times a particular media outlet quotes a US based think tank relative to the number of times US politicians quote that same think tank. The media outlet is then said to have the same political slant as does a politician with the same number of quotes. It is important to note that slant or bias here does not mean inaccurate or false reporting, rather that the media outlet has a preference for one side of the political spectrum relative to the other. This particular measure is likely to be quite robust. In the first instance US politicians are less subject to party discipline than are, say, Australian politicians. US politicians are less likely to vote on strict party-political lines than are Australian politicians.

By observing actual political voting patterns observers are able to estimate reasonable measures of how conservative or progressive any US politician is likely to be. Groseclose and Milyo make use of those objective measures of political slant when determining media bias. The other point to remember is that they make use of think tanks in their study—not individuals who are more likely to change their minds over time or have varying policy positions on different issues. Generally speaking the Groseclose and Milyo analysis finds that the media is quite progressive (in US terms 'liberal') in outlook. In short, they find 'a systematic tendency for the United States media outlets to slant the news to the left'. In particular they report that the media is more centralist relative to the average politician in the US Congress—that is, in ideological space they tend to lie between the average Democrat and the average Republican. Surprisingly, they find that government funded media outlets are less progressive than non-government funded media outlets.

Using a similar method to Groseclose and Milyo, Oliver Latham of the UK-based Centre for Policy Studies finds that the BBC is more likely to quote think tanks that have been referenced by the Guardian newspaper than those referenced by the Daily Telegraph.[29] What is especially interesting is his investigation of 'health warnings' that the BBC provides before referencing a centre-left think tank relative to a centre-right think tank. He reports that centre-left think tanks are far more likely to be labelled as 'independent' or not at all, than centre-right think tanks.

An Australian version of the Groseclose and Milyo paper was published in 2012 by Joshua Gans and Andrew Leigh.[30] They perform a similar analysis to Groseclose and Milyo but rather than look for media citing think tanks and then comparing that to politicians citing those same think tanks, Gans and Leigh look at the media and politicians citing individuals over the period 1996 to 2007. That might seem like a small deviation in the research method—yet it represents a massive reduction in effective sample size. Groseclose and Milyo have 200 think tanks in their sample over a ten-year period—in effect that could mean that hundreds, if not thousands, of individuals may have authored comments that were subsequently quoted by politicians. By contrast, Gans and Leigh initially make use of the *Sydney Morning Herald's* Top 100 Public Intellectuals from 2005. Despite its name that list actually comprises 127 individuals. As they admit, the *Sydney Morning Herald* list significantly under-represents conservative or right-of-centre opinion. To rectify that omission they then add to their list the research staff of the Centre for Independent Studies and the Institute of Public Affairs. The cohort of think tank staff used in the analysis is that cohort employed at the time (in 2007) Gans and Leigh undertook the research for the paper. To the extent that think tank employees tend to be young and staff turnover tends to be high, it is very likely the study under-represents centre-right opinion.

The Gans and Leigh paper suffers from look-back bias and survivorship bias; consequently its results are profoundly flawed. What Gans and Leigh have done is take a list of public intellectuals from 2005 (augmented it with additional individuals from 2007) and then back cast that list of individuals over the period 1996 to 2007. This ignores all those public intellectuals who were active prior to 2005 but were not on the list in 2005 (due to death, or retirement, or some other occurrence). Being mentioned in the Parliament and in the media prior to 2005 is itself a criterion for inclusion onto the list in 2005.[31]

The initial results are problematic. More positive mentions by one party lead to the individual being allocated to that side of the political spectrum. Does anyone really believe that Phillip Adams (26 mentions, 65 per cent Coalition) has politics that are right of centre? Or Eva Cox (9 mentions, 56 per cent Coalition), Germaine Greer (4 mentions, 75 per cent Coalition) or Hugh MacKay (18 mentions, 78 per cent Coalition)? The overall results are also counter-intuitive. Melbourne local ABC radio station 774 is identified as being more pro-Coalition than is the *Australian* newspaper. To be fair, however, neither of those two media outlets is statistically significantly different from the overall neutral position. In fact, only one media outlet is statistically significantly different from the neutral position—according to Gans and Leigh, ABC television news had a right-slant, that is, was pro-Coalition over the period 1996 to 2007. What Gans and Leigh have found is that most (all except one media outlet) media in Australia is unbiased—there is no slant according to their own revised application of the Groseclose and Milyo methodology. That is an interesting result in itself—yet the finding that ABC television news is right-slanted is unconvincing. It is very likely that methodological flaws in the Gans and Leigh paper are driving that result.

In an essay on the state and future of the ABC in *Meanjin* published in 2017, the journalism academic Margaret Simons dismisses the 'ABC is left-wing' argument as being 'a distraction, a falsity and a trap'.[32] Her argument is that while many ABC employees may have personal views that could be described as being 'left-wing' that they are professional in doing their job. Nevertheless, this is hard to square with her subsequent claim that public broadcasting has a positive social role:

> Public media is not fairy dust sprinkled on democracy. Nevertheless, as a component of the mix it represents powerful potential. The ABC, more than any other institution, occupies the space between the private reflections of individual Australians and our capacity as a nation to cohere. In these polarised and fractured times, a strong publicly funded national media organisation holds the possibility that we might not be taken by surprise at the views and life experiences of our fellow citizens—that we will retain some threads to bind us and enable us to talk.

That seems a very optimistic view of the future of public broadcasting, but it's difficult to see how the ABC could play that positive role given its potential biases and limited market share. In any event we have contested a similar argument in the last chapter. Indeed, Simons' argument appears to confirm the very worst fear Uhlmann's critics express, writing that 'those who want to change the country—or those who want to resist change—must deal with the national broadcaster'. Certainly the national broadcaster deals with them. The ABC doesn't just reflect national attitudes, it attempts to mould those attitudes too. Simons again:

> If we see in today's Western politics—in Brexit and in Trump—the legacy of the 1990s, as the losers from globali-

> sation and economic rationalism take out their anger at the ballot box, then the ABC, as a survivor from different times, is an asset as we try to work out the future together.

This is, however, a very particular interpretation on the Brexit vote and Donald Trump's election. For those who welcomed the British withdrawal from the European Union and the 2016 US election result it is clear that, at least in Simons' view, the ABC exists to resist, or somehow ameliorate those democratic impulses. It is not clear that a government agency should exist that attempts to shift the democratic wishes of the population. Given that Simons argues, 'Its job is to connect us, to help maintain some common understandings of who we are, the issues we face and the values we share'.[33] Yet many Australians do not share the values the ABC espouses.

Even former Chairman of the ABC board Maurice Newman admits there is bias at the ABC. In a 2010 speech to the ABC staff Newman made some uncontroversial comments:

> At the ABC, I believe we must reenergise the spirit of enquiry. Be dynamic and challenging—to look for contrary points of view, to ensure that the maverick voice will not be silenced. There should be no public perception that there is such a thing as an 'ABC view'—we must be neither believers nor atheists but agnostics who acknowledge people have a right to make up their own minds.[34]

Newman's speech caused a firestorm. *The Sydney Morning Herald* accused him of 'tread[ing] outside his own area of expertise' and being unfamiliar with the public broadcaster's coverage.[35] Newman reflected on the fall-out from that speech two years later that his 'mistake was to mention climate change'.[36] Newman had taken, as an example, the media coverage of the ClimateGate scandal, suggesting that the media could have held the scientists at the heart of that scandal to greater account.[37] For his trouble Newman was labelled a 'denier', and then in 2012 Robyn Williams, host of *The Science Show*, likened his position to an argument for paedophilia, asbestos, or teenage use of crack cocaine:

> Now what if I told you pedophilia is good for children or that asbestos is an excellent inhalant for those with asthma? Or that smoking crack is a normal part, and a healthy one, of teenage life and to be encouraged? You'd rightly find it outrageous. But there have been similar statements coming out of inexpert mouths again and again in recent times, distorting the science [of climate change].[38]

This response over the issue of climate change, of course, highlights where the political sympathies of the ABC rest. In a paper published by the Institute of Public Affairs in 2014, now Liberal senator James Paterson detailed the results of a content analysis into how the ABC frames Australia's energy technology choices. That paper found that:

> The ABC treats the coal industry poorly, systemically underplaying the economic significance of coal energy generation and focusing its attention on the effect coal may have on the global environment.
>
> It treats the renewable energy industry highly favourably. This favourability is based not only on renewable energy's low carbon emissions profile, but the ABC regularly claims that the economics of renewable energy are also highly favourable.[39]

His conclusion is that the ABC is so biased against fossil fuels that the ABC is effectively campaigning for renewable energy. Furthermore, Paterson found that this bias is so consistent across regions and media platforms that the bias is institutionalised and systemic and not idiosyncratic.

Further evidence of bias can be seen in the ABC's one-sided approach to enforcing its 'editorial standards' in response to public controversy. One of the ABC's premier political shows is the Sunday morning television program *Insiders*, hosted by the former Labor press secretary Barrie Cassidy, consisting of a panel of three journalists who together with Cassidy discuss the politics of the week. The composition of the panel is usually two left-leaning journalists and one right-of-centre journalist. In 2011 the Australian journalist and commentator Glenn Milne was abruptly dropped from the show after publishing an expose in the Australian of then Prime Minister Julia Gillard's association with an individual later accused of fraud. Following a direct intervention by Gillard, the Australian had withdrawn the story and apologised.[40] The ABC then publicly announced that it would no longer have Milne on *Insiders*, despite the fact that Milne had not raised the issue on the program.

Alan Sunderland—Head of Policy at the ABC—justified dropping Milne 'as it was essential that participants could be relied upon not to compromise the ABC's editorial standards'.[41] Yet those very same editorial standards did not prevent the ABC from claiming that Australian Defence Force personal had tortured asylum seekers—allegations that *Media Watch* later admitted were not borne out by the evidence.[42] Nor did they prevent the ABC from broadcasting a photoshopped image of the commentator Chris Kenny abusing an animal, in response to Kenny's argument that ABC funding should be reduced. In the controversy that followed, the head of the ABC's Audience and Consumer Affairs unit considered that it was 'in keeping with the ABC's editorial standards'.[43] ABC editorial standards did not prevent the ABC's Chief Economics Correspondent Emma Alberici from publishing an anti-tax cut opinion piece containing at least nine errors, unreasonable assertions and/or omissions.[44]

ABC hosts have also suggested that other media organisations sack their own conservative employees in response to political trends. After the 2007 election that saw the centre-right Howard government replaced by the centre-left Rudd government, Jon Faine asked the question whether the print media would have a 'cleansing process' to remove those conservative columnists who had 'worn out their usefulness' and who were 'out of step with the result of the election'.[45] *Insiders* also dropped the conservative *Daily Telegraph* columnist Piers Akerman in 2013. His offense was to confirm on-air the existence of rumours relating to the then prime minister's partner circulating around Canberra press gallery journalists. Despite explicitly stating that the rumours were untrue and inappropriate Akerman was subsequently dropped from the show. With this record it is hard to see how the ABC might function as an institution where 'we try to work out the future together'.

5 The case for privatisation

Margaret Simons describes the ABC as 'an immense national asset' with 'a tremendous legacy'. Yet she also tells us that '[c]hange is necessary'.[1] The questions then become 'What change?' and 'How should the ABC be changed?' Having a national asset with a tremendous legacy doesn't mean that we should keep that asset in public ownership. After all Australia has had many such assets—the Commonwealth Bank and Qantas come to mind. Indeed Australia still has those assets, even if the government no longer directly owns them.

What could be done with the ABC?

It is certainly the case that doing nothing and muddling through is very much underrated as a government policy. In the first instance any proposed reforms of the ABC must be demonstrably preferable to the status quo. The ABC is a confused organisation that is not quite a market-failure broadcaster, but is not organised on a commercial basis either. It can either be thought of as a bureaucracy or as a non-profit organisation. It suffers from all the disadvantages of each but doesn't seem to provide any of the benefits of either. This might not matter if lower-cost alternative public policies were not otherwise available. Preserving the status quo suggests that nothing should be done about a government policy that ultimately fails to meet its stated objectives—such as they are—and that does nothing about media bias and crowding out.

Another possibility would be to refine the ABC Charter. In the first instance the ABC could be redesignated to be a market-failure broadcaster. Those audiences and markets that are not otherwise viable could be serviced by the ABC. This approach would be consistent with Adam Smith's view of government intervention—the ABC could be an institution 'in the highest degree advantageous to a great society' but 'of such a nature that the profit could never repay the expense to any individual or small number of individuals'. Yet, as we have argued, it is unclear what a market-failure broadcaster would broadcast in the modern era. It is not obvious that any particular audience or market is not being served or could be served.

By contrast, if the ABC were not to be a dedicated market-failure broadcaster, it could be required to be self-funding, i.e.

commercialised. Here the ABC could be required to finance its activities through advertising revenue much as any other media organisation and then pay dividends to the government. The advantage of this arrangement is that it would address many of the problems created by the ABC—incentives to over-expansion and crowding out would be blunted. It is unclear, however, why commercialisation should be a new status quo, as opposed to simply being a pathway to privatisation. At this point the government, as owner, would have to evaluate whether the policy objectives of a wholly owned ABC paying dividends would be achieved as opposed to a partially or totally privatised ABC paying company tax and/or dividends.

If we assume for argument's sake that there are good reasons for government intervention in the media market, that still does not require a government-owned media organisation. There is no reason why government could not simply contract with private firms for specific services. The government could either contract for specific programming or contract an entire service. Depending what the government chose to contract there may be no need for the ABC to exist at all. The Australian government has attempted this approach before. In 2010 the Australia Network—a media service targeting south-east Asia and the Pacific previously operated by the ABC under contract—was put out to tender. It is well worth recalling that this activity is already required of the ABC under its existing Charter. After some internal debate and a rather confused tender process where Sky News twice won the tender, the Gillard government awarded the tender permanently to the ABC.

Notwithstanding this messy political tender process the question remains why the government should have put a service out to tender when it already had an entire agency whose function is to provide that very service. Putting parts of the ABC out to tender raises the question why the entire ABC is not, or cannot, be put out to tender. Indeed, why the entirety of the ABC is not a tendered-out service was a question first posed in 1932:

> I do not think that the broadcasting programmes will be improved under the proposed commission control any more than under some system similar to that in existence at present, but on a more competitive basis. If the Government were to invite applications for the broadcasting of programmes, I am satisfied that many associations would be willing to conduct an improved service at a cost much lower than that operating today.[2]

A further option would be to reform the governance of the ABC. It is very clear that there are profound problems at the ABC board level. Margaret Simons writes that:

> The ABC board is opaque. It has had quality members as well as a distressingly high proportion of ratbags. One hopes it engages in strategic planning, but insiders have suggested that for the last decade or so, various political ideologues on the board have used the precious time to chew over the predictable chestnuts, then signed off on strategies coming from management.

We suspect that we disagree as to who have been 'ratbags' and 'ideologues' on the ABC board, but the fact remains that the board is opaque and does not seem to constrain the ABC or its management. From the outside it appears that the only meaningful function of the ABC board is to select the managing director.

Harvard University's Michael Jensen has argued that there are four mechanisms to exert control over an organisation when managerial decision-making deviates from optimal societal control.[3] These forces are: capital markets; legal, regulatory and political controls; factor and product markets; and internal control mechanisms such as boards of directors. The ABC seems, more or less, able to circumvent all of these mechanisms. It is funded directly by government and so is not constrained by capital markets, its Charter is not enforceable in the legal system and politicians seem loath to seriously confront the ABC, it has no profit motive so product market performance provides no discipline, and it is freed from public sector employment salary restrictions in order to compete in factor markets. The ABC board of directors is the only mechanism to provide any discipline to the ABC. Yet we know that does not happen.

There are four obvious solutions to a lack of effective governance. First the government could introduce mechanisms that hold the board to account. That would mean making the board legally accountable for delivering the ABC Charter. Conversely the ABC could be brought under democratic control and have to report to the minister of communications. The minister in turn would be answerable to the electorate at the ballot box for the performance of the ABC. Alternatively, commercialisation of the ABC would expose it to discipline from factor and product markets. There is one policy, however, that would simultaneously expose the ABC to discipline from all four of Michael Jensen's disciplinary forces: privatisation.

Privatising the ABC

Privatisation is the transfer of ownership rights in state-owned enterprises to the private sector. Journalist and political science professor Peter van Onselen has summarised the argument for the privatisation of the ABC as follows:

> The ABC should be privatised to save the taxpayer the more than $1 billion it costs each year to run, to reap a one-off injection of revenue from the sale price to help retire government debt, and to remove a government-funded goliath that is interfering with the market in the media landscape.[4]

To be fair, many Australians are ideologically opposed to privatisation and find van Onselen's argument unconvincing. Yet he is quite correct to point to the fact that a $1 billion government program imposes costs on the Australian community at a time when government revenue is precarious and public debt growing. Simultaneously arguments to maintain public broadcasting are weak and alternative reforms are unlikely to address those problems. There are both good and bad reasons to privatise the ABC. One bad reason would be to privatise the ABC as some sort of punishment for its political views. One Nation threatened to advocate cutting the ABC budget by some $600 million over four years in retaliation for reporting into One Nation's internal squabbling. Tony Walker, formerly a journalist at the *Australian Financial Review*, sets out political criticism of the ABC in recent years:

> If there has been a consistent theme in multiple conversations in recent months with Coalition figures, from senior ministers down, it is that the ABC promotes a worldview inimical to conservative viewpoints on issues like climate change and asylum-seeker policy.[5]

On the same day Dennis Shanahan, writing in the *Weekend Australian*, had a more damning assessment:[6]

> The politics of the current furore are undoubtedly fuelled by the Coalition, particularly Liberal MPs and ministers, wanting to embark on cultural retribution against the ABC; but also by the government's intent to lay the groundwork for justifying cuts to the ABC through either an efficiency drive or dividend, or by permanently axing the ABC's $223 million Australia Network broadcasting service into Asia … There is a recognition within the government that previous attempts to change the culture of the ABC have failed. But there is also a recognition and frustration that through a lack of normal and proper editorial and management processes, the ABC seemed determined to ignore the reality of a change of government and has not taken real steps to ensure its guidelines on impartiality and accuracy were enforced.

Now neither Shanahan nor Walker canvassed the notion of privatisation, but they do point to a dissatisfaction with the ABC and Shanahan points to a desire for some sort of retribution. While the desire to punish one's political enemies may be very human, it is illiberal and incompatible with a society that operates under the rule of law. Good reasons need to be articulated to justify privatisation.

Similarly there are bad reasons not to privatise government-owned assets. Many of these reasons are set out in a 2000 book, published (perhaps with a small tinge of self-interest) by ABC Books. In *Privatisation: Sell off or sell out?* Bob Walker and Betty Walker set out a long list of criticisms of privatisation.[7] Privatisation, apparently, has produced massive wealth transfers within the community, conferred privileges on insiders, led to the loss of services to the community, led to loss of jobs in government, led to spurious claims of savings to taxpayers, risked the marginalisation of rural communities, seen government-owned state-based monopolies dismantled, created powerful private monopolies, contributed to environmental damage, and eroded public sector accountability. Many of these objections are more properly levied at government-owned bureaucracies and enterprises, who are subsidised and protected from the more effective discipline of the competitive market. But what makes their everything-but-the-kitchen-sink argument even harder to evaluate is this admission made on the 7.30 Report that they had 'joined the growing proportion of Australians buying shares'.[8] It seems the attraction of the share ownership society is more than enough to subvert ideological opposition to the privatisation process.

Similarly weak arguments against privatisation have been offered by the former Coalition Treasurer Joe Hockey. On the ABC's *Q&A* program in 2013, Hockey was asked by host Tony Jones whether the Coalition was considering the privatisation of the ABC. His response was that 'The ABC is not for sale. It doesn't make a profit does it, Tony? It is a cost centre, so it is not worth anything for sale. So, no, it is not for sale.'[9] But the ABC could be worth a substantial sum of money on the market, if the government were ever to make the effort to ensure that the ABC were profitable. And of course privatisation would lead to cost savings of over $1 billion that Australian taxpayers are currently required to pay for the ABC's services. Hockey proffered another argument in response to a question at a function at the Institute of Public Affairs two years later: 'It employs a few people in my electorate and a lot of people in my electorate actually watch it.'[10] This is pragmatic, but hardly principled.

There are sensible, albeit theoretical, arguments for state-owned enterprise. Indeed the idea that government could own the 'commanding heights' of the economy, if not all enterprise, was a common and popular notion for much of the 20th century. In one sense the biggest economic debate of the 20th century was not between Friedrich Hayek and John Maynard Keynes over macroeconomic policy, but rather between Hayek and Oskar Lange about whether government ownership could outperform private ownership.[11] The theoretical arguments for state-owned enterprise can be superficially compelling. The standard market-failure literature suggests that markets will misallocate resources due to factors such as natural monopoly, various externalities, and asymmetric information. In this framework, government can intervene and improve the allocation of resources, leading to superior outcomes. Of course, observers often think it enough to simply point to some apparent market failure without considering whether government intervention will actually improve on those outcomes. We have argued, however, that the ABC is not a market failure broadcaster.

The best argument for the ABC is that it already exists. This is not a trivial consideration. According to David Sappington and Joseph Stiglitz, privatisation should only occur when the market would perform as well as a benevolent government.[12] That observation, however, has led William Megginson—the foremost academic expert on privatisation—to remark that if governments were benevolent, there would be no need for them to privatise.[13]

There is, however, one argument that relates to the so-called equity-risk premium that is worth examining. Some economists argue that real world equity markets are associated with imperfections that result in the required rates of return being higher than they otherwise should be. There are practical consequences to what would otherwise be an esoteric academic debate.[14] If government did not have to pay those higher rates of return of its cost of capital then state-owned enterprise could enjoy a lower cost of capital than do private sector counterparts. As economists Simon Grant and John Quiggin explain, 'If there is no efficiency loss associated with public ownership, the expected marginal return to public investment … dominates the expected marginal return to private equity … [and] an expansion of public investment is desirable' (emphasis added).[15] At face value, that seems to be a powerful argument. As long as government ownership per se doesn't impact on efficiency, government ownership can be cheaper than private ownership. When stated in those terms, however, it is clear that the Grant–Quiggin view is a violation of the famous Modigliani–Miller theorems of corporate finance. The cost of capital is a function of the riskiness of the investment projects being undertaken, and not a function of the ownership structure of the firm. Government ownership is likely to impact upon efficiency and there are no free lunches.

There are two lesser-known arguments in favour of state-owned enterprises. They can be used to pursue social objectives such as employing minorities or undertaking investment in remote areas. We have already raised some objections to this argument in Chapter 3. Alternatively, with a state-owned enterprise the government might be able to overcome principal–agent problems by better controlling management than diverse and dispersed shareholders would be able to. Yet the inability of the ABC board to control that organisation seems to suggest this explanation is more wishful thinking than actual reality.

Nevertheless, it is the empirical record on privatisation that is decisive. Megginson has summed up that record as: '[a] lmost all studies that examine post-privatization changes in output, efficiency, profitability, capital investment spending, and leverage document significant increases in the first four and significant declines in leverage'.[16] As a general principle, all governments with significant state-owned assets should pursue a policy of privatisation.

Argument for privatising the ABC go well beyond a general principle about the desirability of private enterprise over state owned enterprise. The arguments for public broadcasting are poor. A government policy exists that cannot be justified on its merits—apart the fact that it exists already. At the same time we know the costs of that policy are non-trivial. We also know that observers who are generally supportive of the ABC recognise that there are problems in the organisation that need to be addressed. Similarly, not all ABC critics embrace the privatisation agenda. While the former Australian opinion page editor Rebecca Weisser argues that the ABC is 'controlled by an unrepresentative clique', she nonetheless has written of the ABC's national purpose: 'Only a public broadcaster can play this crucial role in the life of the nation. Yes, it requires public subsidy. So do the arts and sports. Those advocating privatisation suspect it would fail, but don't care'.[17]

What would privatisation look like?

Weisser is correct: it is one thing to argue that public broadcasting is poor public policy. It is quite another thing to argue that the government should simply discontinue that policy.

William Megginson has argued, 'it now seems clear that private ownership is superior to public ownership of commercial enterprise in almost all realistic business settings'.[18] The far more important issue is the nature of that private ownership. The ownership of the ABC could be either concentrated or diffuse. At present the ownership is concentrated—the ABC is owned by a single entity, the Commonwealth government. As much as some might want to argue that the Australian public own the ABC and that there are some 23 million shareholders, that romantic notion of state ownership is hard to defend.

One possibility is that the federal government could sell the ABC to another single entity or consortium. It is easy to imagine that an Australian, or international, mogul might be interested in acquiring the ABC. Alternatively the federal government could sell the ABC on the stock market, offering shares to Australian citizens and institutional shareholders much in the way that several other previously state-owned enterprises were sold. This would transform the current concentrated ownership structure to a diffuse ownership structure. The ABC could be sold in tranches with a partial privatisation leading to a full privatisation over time, and so on. It is very likely this latter approach would be more politically acceptable to a government than selling it to a single purchaser.

Of course, selling the ABC requires a valuation of the ABC. Clearly the ABC is valuable—but how valuable? How long would it take to transform an organisation that has almost no commercial income to one that is reliant on generating income in order to cover its costs? The government may find that it cannot realise the ABC's value. That, however, does not mean that the ABC should remain in public ownership—just that the ABC should not be sold in this manner. An alternative approach might be to give the ABC away. The third tranche of Telstra, for example, was transferred to the Future Fund. To the extent that the Future Fund exists to finance the superannuation liabilities of the federal public service, a large part of Telstra was given to public servants. The ABC could be given to the Future Fund. Of course, that does not address any of the commercial problems the ABC would then face.

Our view is that the ABC should be given away to Australian citizens or group of citizens on some pro rata basis—equal shares per head, or share of income tax paid, or welfare benefits consumed, or any other formula deemed equitable and politically palatable. The ABC could be given away to the ABC's current and past employees. Again this could be done on some pro rata basis. This achieves two goals: it effects the privatisation, and vests control of the new private firm with those who have the most incentive for it to succeed. Many employees would of course choose to trade their shares and take their windfall gains. ABC employees are the people who have built up the ABC's brand value (such as it is) and the people best placed to realise any value within the ABC. The employees as shareholders would have a strong incentive to realise efficiencies and develop and grow revenue streams.

How would the ABC self-finance after privatisation? This is first and foremost an entrepreneurial question. Nevertheless, there are several obvious revenue streams that could be exploited. For example, the various Australian governments might still require services provided by the ABC. One such service might be emergency broadcasting. There is no reason why the now-private ABC could not tender for that function. Regular advertising could sustain the ABC. A number of commentators have argued that donations to media organisations should be treated as tax deductable as donations to charities and social science research organisations are today.[19] This proposal for the existing ABC staff members to become shareholders and finance the ABC through the realisation of its value and tax-deductable donations would meet all of Weisser's concerns. The ABC would not be 'controlled by an unrepresentative clique', it would still be privileged in the taxation system, but not financed by the taxpayer (as would every other not-for-profit media outlet). We expect that the ABC in this structure would very quickly adopt positions in its programming and political attitudes that cater for market demand rather than the political preferences of the staff.

The single largest impediment to privatising the ABC is public opinion. While the actual viewership and listenership numbers suggest that most Australians are somewhat indifferent to the ABC, the idea of the ABC is popular, and privatisation as a policy is unpopular. Of course, what people say in response to a general question on a survey and how they react to specific policy proposals is often very different. Privatisation is also likely to interact poorly with at least three of economist Bryan Caplan's four voter biases that lead democracies to make poor economic decisions.[20] Anti-market bias underestimates the economic benefits of markets. Anti-foreign bias undervalues interactions with foreigners. The make-work bias undervalues labour conservation (or productivity improvements). Finally, the pessimism bias overestimates the severity of economic problems. Criticisms of privatisation often revolve around the employment consequences and the selling of 'national icons' to foreigners. By definition, privatisation is making use of the market mechanism. Those voters who suffer from Caplan's biases are likely to oppose privatisation.

When the Menzies government sold its half-share of the Commonwealth Oil Refinery to the then Anglo-Iranian Oil Company (now British Petroleum) in 1952 the Labor opposition opposed the sale saying the price was too low, and that it would undermine national security.[21] The arguments opposing privatisation have not changed much since, and we still hear those justifications for government involvement in the private economy. To use Thomas Sowell's terminology, there exists a conflict of visions in the privatisation debate between statist propaganda that citizens have been exposed to over long periods of time and the lived experience.[22] The lived experience is that privatisation as a policy has been successful, while the propaganda goes to the core of political debate. Privatisation as a policy raises questions about the role and function of the state generally and, in particular, the role of the state in the economy. That these are deep and important questions is no reason not to raise them.

One final objection to this proposal is that the Commonwealth would not realise the value of the ABC if it simply gifted the ABC to current and past employees. That objection, however, ignores the role of taxation. In the case of the giveaway to ABC employees, the government would begin to collect income tax revenue from ABC employees. At present the Commonwealth collects tax revenue from Australian taxpayers and then makes an appropriation to the ABC—the ABC pays its employees who in turn pay tax back to the government. Post-privatisation any tax revenue the government received from ABC employees would constitute a net gain in revenue and not simply represent churn. In addition, as ABC employees—now shareholders—sold off their shareholdings in the ABC they would pay capital gains tax. Having received the shares at zero-price the ABC employees would be liable to pay tax on the entire capital gain due to their value-add (subject, of course, to the capital gain discount of 50 per cent) and at their marginal tax rate.

In this sense the privatisation of the ABC would proceed much like higher education is currently funded. The new owners would receive their shares at zero-price (effectively a zero-interest loan) and only pay for them when they disposed of the shares and only then if the shares had increased in value. The proceeds of the privatisation would be realised over time and would not constitute a 'sugar-hit' to the budget. Nor can the privatisation be characterised as a stunt to balance the budget in the short term. Rather, it is a program to establish a newly-private ABC on a firm footing, vesting it with a cohort of new owners who have the most interest in making it a commercial success.

6 Conclusion

Privatisation is not alien to Australian broadcasting and wireless history. The public-private partnership AWA, capitalised by the Commonwealth in order to build a wireless telegraphy link between London and Australia, was privatised by the Menzies government in 1951. AWA's thirty years of government part-ownership were not entirely happy. As the communications scholar Jock Given writes, 'technology changed and the uses of wireless expanded into areas where the Commonwealth was less enthusiastic about being a major shareholder'.[1] AWA's sale was described as the first move in the Menzies government's platform of 'desocialising instrumentalities where possible'.[2]

Australia has experienced another wave of 'desocialisation' since the opening up of Australia's trade and financial sector in the 1970s and 1980s. Governments have come to understand that the benefits of state ownership are harder to realise within the strictures of bureaucracy and party politics, and that the disadvantages of market competition are not as significant as their forebears may have imagined. Those governments also understood that technological change and innovion meant that consumers (and the economy in general) were more likely to benefit when firms were exposed to the market. One of the key drivers of the deregulation of banking in the early 1980s, for example, was the possibilities that new technologies like automatic teller machines, the expansion of credit card and EFTPOS networks, and telephone banking had for waking up the sleepy banking industry. But those changes pale in comparison to the technological changes experienced by the media industry.

In the space of a decade, we have come to experience media not as it is 'pushed' to us—only enjoying content that has been chosen for us, curated by others, and provided at a fixed time and in a fixed quantity—but as we 'pull' it to ourselves—bingeing on our favourite television series that is streamed in high-definition to our internet-enabled televisions; resuming where we left off on our mobile phones as we train in to work; listening to podcasts that revisit the latest episode; forever scanning blogs and social media for the next big thing. The move from push media to pull media has been long coming. But now that it is here it has heavy implications for the regulatory and institutional framework that governs Australia's legacy media.

In the new comparative economics approach that has informed this book, technological change shifts the relative dictatorship and disorder costs of state and market institutional control respectively. Technological change can make government activity less costly and less harmful to liberties. Conversely, technological change can reduce the likelihood of market failure or any other harms caused by free market institutions. When the new comparative economics approach is filtered through the Austrian economics framework of subjective value and methodological individualism, it is also clear that technological change reduces public perceptions of those costs.[3]

Public broadcasting is not the only media policy change that ought to be made in the light of these technological changes. For example, reforms ought to be made to spectrum licensing and allocation, intellectual property, and laws constraining freedom of speech and expression. Other regulatory requirements, such as Australian content standards and quotas, are archaic in a global internet media market and ought to be repealed. Yet the last decade of regulatory reform in media has been slow and halting. On the one hand it has held legacy firms back from making needed changes. On the other hand it has slowed entrepreneurial activity from challenging those firms. It might be objected that these problems are a good reason for a healthy, and well-funded, public broadcaster. But as we have shown, the ABC is more a cause than a consequence of weaknesses in the Australian media industry.

The ABC is a dominant protected player, established to resolve problems of media scarcity and wireless economics that are no longer relevant. It is large bureaucracy focused on the maintenance of its own privileged position. It is a large participant in the political process that is able to set the political agenda and frame issues in ways which its disproportionately left-leaning staff favour. Its policy rationales for existence are either anachronistic thanks to technological change or could be more efficiently supplied through competitive markets. Finally, it is a billion-dollar drain on the Commonwealth government purse. The ABC should be privatised and freed to flourish in the new media marketplace.

Appendix: The ABC Charter

The ABC Charter appears in section 6 of the Australian Broadcasting Corporation Act (1983):

(1) The functions of the Corporation are:

(a) to provide within Australia innovative and comprehensive broadcasting services of a high standard as part of the Australian broadcasting system consisting of national, commercial and community sectors and, without limiting the generality of the foregoing, to provide:

(i) broadcasting programs that contribute to a sense of national identity and inform and entertain, and reflect the cultural diversity of, the Australian community; and

(ii) broadcasting programs of an educational nature;

(b) to transmit to countries outside Australia broadcasting programs of news, current affairs, entertainment and cultural enrichment that will:

(i) encourage awareness of Australia and an international understanding of Australian attitudes on world affairs; and

(ii) enable Australian citizens living or travelling outside Australia to obtain information about Australian affairs and Australian attitudes on world affairs; and

(ba) to provide digital media services; and

(c) to encourage and promote the musical, dramatic and other performing arts in Australia.

(2) In the provision by the Corporation of its broadcasting services within Australia:

(a) the Corporation shall take account of:

(i) the broadcasting services provided by the commercial and community sectors of the Australian broadcasting system;

(ii) the standards from time to time determined by the ACMA in respect of broadcasting services;

(iii) the responsibility of the Corporation as the provider of an independent national broadcasting service to provide a balance between broadcasting programs of wide appeal and specialized broadcasting programs;

(iv) the multicultural character of the Australian community; and

(v) in connection with the provision of broadcasting programs of an educational nature—the responsibilities of the States in relation to education; and

(b) the Corporation shall take all such measures, being measures consistent with the obligations of the Corporation under paragraph (a), as, in the opinion of the Board, will be conducive to the full development by the Corporation of suitable broadcasting programs.

(3) The functions of the Corporation under subsection (1) and the duties imposed on the Corporation under subsection (2) constitute the Charter of the Corporation.

(4) Nothing in this section shall be taken to impose on the Corporation a duty that is enforceable by proceedings in a court.

Notes

Introduction

1 Commonwealth Parliamentary Debates (CPD), House of Representatives, 10 March 1932, p. 972.
2 A.W. Dobbie & Co Ltd, *The Advertiser*, 18 June 1932, p. 8.
3 J Eggleston, *The Guyra Argus*, 28 July 1938, p. 5.
4 Cited in Lesley Johnson, *The Unseen voice : a cultural study of early Australian radio* (London: Routledge, 1988), 87.
5 CPD, House of Representatives, 28 March 1932, p. 91.
6 Julian Fitzgerald, *On message: political communications of*

Australian prime ministers 1901—2014. Mawson: Clareville Press (2014), 140.

7 Deloitte, *Media Consumer Survey 2016: Australian media and digital preferences* (2016).

8 *Media Consumer Survey 2016: The Australian Cut, Hyper connectivity: Clever consumption* (2016).

9 Harry Tucker, 'This is how many people use Snapchat, LinkedIn, Twitter and Facebook in Australia,' *Business Insider Australia*, 31 March 2016.

10 Deloitte, *Media Consumer Survey 2016: Australian media and digital preferences*

11 CPD, House of Representatives, 10 March 1932, p. 978.

12 Frederick Wasser, *Veni, vidi, video: the Hollywood empire and the VCR* (Austin: University of Texas Press,, 2001), 87.

13 Kenneth Stanley Inglis, *Whose ABC? : the Australian Broadcasting Corporation 1983-2006* (Melbourne: Black Inc., 2006); *This is the ABC: the Australian Broadcasting Commission, 1932-1983* (Carlton: Melbourne University Press 1983); Alan Thomas, *Broadcast and be damned: the ABC's first two decades* (Carlton: Melbourne University Press, 1980).

14 Royal Commission on Wireless, *Report* (The Parliament of the Commonwealth of Australia, 1927).

15 Joint Committee on Wireless Broadcasting, *Report* (The Parliament of the Commonwealth of Australia, 1942).

16 Committee of Review of the Australian Broadcasting Commission, *ABC in Review: National Broadcasting in the 1980s* (Canberra: Australian Government Publishing Service, 1981).

17 Department of Transport and Communications, *Review of national broadcasting policy* (Canberra: Australian Government Publishing Service, 1988).

18 Bob Mansfield, *The challenge of a better ABC* (Canberra: Australian Government Publishing Service, 1997).

19 KPMG, *Funding Adequacy and Efficiency Review* (2006); Department of Communications, *ABC and SBS Efficiency Study: Draft Report* (2014).

20 Glyn Davis, *Breaking up the ABC* (Sydney: Allen & Unwin, 1988), 21.

21 *Ibid.*, 138.

22 Simeon Djankov et al., 'The new comparative economics,' *Journal of comparative economics* 31, no. 4 (2003); Andrei Shleifer, *The failure of judges and the rise of regulators* (Cambridge: MIT Press, 2012). This approach has been applied to a diverse range of policy questions, for example, see Chris Berg, 'Safety and soundness: an economic history of prudential bank regulation in Australia, 1893-2008' PhD Thesis (RMIT University, 2016); Chris Berg and Sinclair Davidson, 'Section 18C, Human Rights, and Media Reform: An Institutional Analysis of the 2011-13 Australian Free Speech Debate,' *Agenda: a Journal of Policy Analysis and Reform* 23, no. 1 (2016); 'Media Regulation: A Critique of Finkelstein and Tiffen,' (2015); Sinclair Davidson, *Productivity enhancing regulatory reform, Australia Adjusting: Optimising national prosperity* (2013); 'Environmental protest: an economics of regulation approach,' *Australian Environment Review* 29, no. 10 (2014); Sinclair Davidson and Jason Potts, 'Social costs and the institutions of innovation policy,' (2015); 'A new institutional approach to innovation policy,' *Australian Economic Review* 49, no. 2 (2016); Darcy WE Allen, 'The Subjective Political Economy of Innovation Policy,' (2016); Darcy WE Allen and Chris Berg, 'Subjective Political Economy,' N*ew Perspectives on Political Economy* 13 no. 1-2: 19-40; Trent MacDonald, 'Theory of unbundled

and non-territorial governance: studies in evolutionary political economy' PhD Thesis (RMIT University, 2015).

23 Simeon Djankov et al., 'Who owns the media?,' *Journal of Law and Economics* 46 (2003).

24 Australia Broadcasting Commission Act 1932, s. 16.

25 Sinclair Davidson 'The ABC Charter is not 'Law'', *Catallaxy Files*, 11 October, 2016, http://catallaxyfiles.com/2016/10/11/the-abc-charter-is-not-law/.

26 Australian Broadcasting Corporation, *Annual Report* (2016).

The origins of public broadcasting

1 Bridget Griffen-Foley, *Changing stations: the story of Australian commercial radio* (Sydney: UNSW Press, 2009); 'The birth of a hybrid: the shaping of the Australian radio industry,' *Radio Journal: International Studies in Broadcast & Audio Media* 2, no. 3 (2004).

2 Ann Mozley Moyal, *Clear across Australia: a history of telecommunications* (Melbourne, Vic: Nelson, 1984); R. W. Home, 'Threlfall, Sir Richard (1861–1932),' (Carlton, Victoria: Melbourne University Publishing, 1990).

3 Cited in Sungook Hong, *Wireless: from Marconi's black-box to the audion*, (Cambridge: MIT Press, 2001), 8.

4 Moyal, *Clear across Australia: a history of telecommunications.*

5 Ross Curnow, 'The origins of Australian broadcasting, 1900–23,' in *Initiative and Organisation*, ed. Ian Bedford and Ross Curnow (Melbourne: F.W. Cheshire, 1963).

6 CPD, Senate, 2 August 1905, p. 464.

7 Curnow, 'The origins of Australian broadcasting, 1900–23,' 53.

8 For the contest between Marconi and Telefunken see

Michael Friedewald, 'Telefunken vs. Marconi, or the Race for Wireless Telegraphy at Sea, 1896-1914,' SSRN (2012).

9 Curnow, 'The origins of Australian broadcasting, 1900–23.'

10 Moyal, *Clear across Australia: a history of telecommunications*, 113.

11 Jock Given, 'A 50/50 proposition: public-private partnerships in Australian communications,' *Media International Australia* 129, no. 1 (2008).

12 Curnow, 'The origins of Australian broadcasting, 1900–23.'

13 *Ibid.*, 98.

14 Ron Langhans, *The First Twelve Months of Radio Broadcasting in Australia: 1923-1924* (Historical Radio Society of Australia, 2013).

15 Griffen-Foley, 'The birth of a hybrid: the shaping of the Australian radio industry.'

16 H. May Trott Fessenden, *Fessenden, builder of tomorrows* (New York: Coward-McCann, 1940), 153; Susan J. Douglas, *Inventing American broadcasting, 1899-1922* (Baltimore: Johns Hopkins University Press, 1987).

17 Jesse Walker, *Rebels on the air: an alternative history of radio in America* (New York: New York University Press,, 2001).

18 Douglas, *Inventing American broadcasting, 1899-1922*, 312; Simon James Potter, *Broadcasting empire the BBC and the British world, 1922-1970* (Oxford: Oxford University Press,, 2012).

19 Asa Briggs, *The history of broadcasting in the United Kingdom* (London: Oxford University Press, 1961), vol. 1, 64.

20 J. C. W. Reith, *Broadcast over Britain* (London: Hodder and Stoughton, 1924), 81.

21 Thomas W. Hazlett, *The Political Spectrum: the tumultuous liberation of wireless technology, from Herbert Hoover to the smartphone* (New Haven and London: Yale University Press, 2017).
22 Briggs, *The history of broadcasting in the United Kingdom*, v. 1, 73.
23 Chris Berg, *In defence of freedom of speech: from Ancient Greece to Andrew Bolt*, Monographs on Western civilisation (Melbourne; Subiaco: Institute of Public Affairs; Mannkal Economic Education Foundation, 2012); David J Brennan, 'Printing in England and Broadcasting in Australia: A Comparative Study of Regulatory Impulse,' *Adelaide Law Review* 22 (2000).
24 Briggs, T*he history of broadcasting in the United Kingdom*, 100.
25 Paddy Scannell, 'Public service broadcasting: the history of a concept,' *Understanding television* (1990).
26 Reith, *Broadcast over Britain; Memorandum of Information on the Scope and Conduct of the Broadcasting Service* (Caversham, Reading: BBC Written Archive, 1925).
27 Potter, B*roadcasting empire the BBC and the British world, 1922-1970;* Michael Bailey, 'Rethinking public service broadcasting: the historical limits to publicness,' in *Media and public spheres* (Springer, 2007).
28 Royal Commission on Wireless, *Report*; 'Wireless Commission', *The Age*, 26 July 1927
29 Thomas, *Broadcast and be damned : the ABC's first two decades.*
30 Inglis, *This is the ABC: the Australian Broadcasting Commission, 1932-1983.*
31 CPD, House of Representatives, 29 October 1931, p. 1331.
32 Thomas, *Broadcast and be damned: the ABC's first two decades*, 12.

33 'Broadcasting', *The Sydney Morning Herald*, 21 January 1932, p. 10.
34 CPD, House of Representatives, 9 March 1932, p. 841.
35 Geoffrey Sawer, *Australian federal politics and law, 1929-1949* (Melbourne: Melbourne University Press, 1963), 54.
36 GA Roberts, 'Business interests and the formation of the ABC,' *Politics* 7, no. 2 (1972).
37 CPD, House of Representatives, 3 May 1932, p. 268.
38 See for instance CPD, House of Representatives, 8 and 9 August 1946, p. 4098.
39 Inglis, *This is the ABC : the Australian Broadcasting Commission, 1932-1983.*
40 Cited in Thomas, *Broadcast and be damned: the ABC's first two decades*, 158.
41 Australian Broadcasting Bill 1948, section 22(b)
42 'ABC Service', *Daily Mercury*, 14 February 1947, p. 2.
43 Inglis, T*his is the ABC: the Australian Broadcasting Commission, 1932-1983*; Thomas, *Broadcast and be damned: the ABC's first two decades;* Michael Francis Dixon, *Inside the ABC: a piece of Australian history* (Melbourne: Hawthorn Press, 1975). For an overview of the Chifley government's radicalism, see Tim Battin, 'Keynesianism, Socialism, and Labourism, and the Role of Ideas in Labor Ideology,' *Labour History*, no. 66 (1994).
44 Inglis, *This is the ABC: the Australian Broadcasting Commission, 1932-1983.*
45 R. W. Burns, *British television: the formative years* (London: P. Peregrinus in association with the Science Museum, 1986).
46 *Television: an international history of the formative years* (London: Institution of Engineering and Technology, 1998).
47 CPD, House of Representatives, 9 March 1932, p. 845.

48 Joint Committee on Wireless Broadcasting, *Report*
49 'Television later', *Maryborough Chronicle*, 8 April 1948, p. 6.
50 CPD, House of Representatives, 24 November 1948, p. 3453.
51 Inglis, *This is the ABC: the Australian Broadcasting Commission, 1932-1983*.
52 National Archives of Australia, A4639, 51
53 Inglis, *This is the ABC: the Australian Broadcasting Commission, 1932-1983*.
54 Robert Albon and Franco Papandrea, *Media regulation in Australia and the public interest*, Current issues (Melbourne: Institute of Public Affairs, 1998); Richard Allsop, 'How government holds back technological change,' *IPA Review* (2014).
55 Royal Commission on Television, *Report* (Canberra: Commonwealth of Australia, 1954).
56 Ibid., 55.
57 Albert Moran, 'Some beginnings for Australian television,' *Continuum: Journal of Media & Cultural Studies* 4, no. 2 (1991).
58 Cited in Inglis, *This is the ABC: the Australian Broadcasting Commission, 1932-1983*, 195.
59 Ann Curthoys, 'Television before television,' *Continuum: Journal of Media & Cultural Studies* 4, no. 2 (1991): 167.
60 F. J. Green, *Australian broadcasting: a report on the structure of the Australian broadcasting system and associated matters* (Canberra: Postal and Telecommunications Department, 1977).
61 National Archives of Australia, A12909, 2987
62 Committee of Review of the Australian Broadcasting Commission, *ABC in Review: National Broadcasting in the 1980s*
63 Cited in *ibid.*, 129.

64 *Ibid.*, 23-24.
65 Department of Transport and Communications, *Review of national broadcasting policy*
66 Allan Brown, 'Australian public broadcasting under review: the Mansfield report on the ABC,' *Canadian Journal of Communication* 26, no. 1 (2001).
67 Mansfield, *The challenge of a better ABC.*

Why does the public need a broadcaster?

1 Harvey Joshua Levin, *Fact and fancy in television regulation : an economic study of policy alternatives* (New York: Russell Sage Foundation, 1980), 3.
2 Cited in Thomas, *Broadcast and be damned : the ABC's first two decades*, 18.
3 Kenneth A Shepsle, 'Bureaucratic drift, coalitional drift, and time consistency: A comment on Macey,' *Journal of Law, Economics, & Organization* 8, no. 1 (1992); David Epstein and Sharyn O'Halloran, 'Administrative procedures, information, and agency discretion,' *American Journal of Political Science* (1994).
4 Albon and Papandrea, *Media regulation in Australia and the public interest*; C. Edwin Baker, *Media, markets, and democracy* (Cambridge: Cambridge University Press, 2002).
5 The discussion about public goods draws on Sinclair Davidson, 'Why have an ABC at all?,' *ABC The Drum*, 20 December 2011.
6 Adam Smith, *An inquiry into the nature and causes of the wealth of nations* (Chicago: University of Chicago Press, 1976).
7 Independent Review Panel, *The Future Funding of the BBC* (Department for Culture, Media and Sport, 1999), 10.

8 Dan Sabbagh, 'ABC director general Mark Scott gives his perspective on the BBC's travails,' *Guardian*, 16 May 2011.
9 Mark Day, 'Scott's talk of ABC being a market failure is cheap,' *The Australian*, 23 May 2011.
10 CPD, Senate, Environment and Communications Legislation Committee, 5 May 2016, p. 127.
11 Australian Broadcasting Corporation, *Submission to the House of Representatives Standing Committee on Communications and the Arts Inquiry into the importance of public and commercial broadcasting, online content and live production to rural and regional Australia, including the arts, news and other services* (Sydney: Australian Broadcasting Corporation, 2016).
12 Dominic White, 'Mistake or two but still our ABC, says chair,' *The Australian Financial Review*, 20 December 2014.
13 Christopher Pleatsikas and David Teece, 'The analysis of market definition and market power in the context of rapid innovation,' *International Journal of Industrial Organization* 19, no. 5 (2001): 667.
14 Jonathan Dörr et al., 'Music as a Service as an Alternative to Music Piracy?,' *Business & Information Systems Engineering* 5, no. 6 (2013).
15 Heather Mac Donald, 'Great Courses, Great Profits,' *City Journal*, no. Summer (2011).
16 Friedrich August Hayek, 'The use of knowledge in society,' *The American Economic Review* (1945).
17 Christopher J. Coyne and Peter T. Leeson, *Media, development and institutional change*, New thinking in political economy (Cheltenham: Edward Elgar, 2009), 162.
18 Levin, *Fact and fancy in television regulation : an economic study of policy alternatives*. See also Bruce M Owen, 'The

economic view of programming,' Journal of Communication 28, no. 2 (1978).

19 Denis McQuail, *Media performance : mass communication and the public interest* (London: Sage, 1992), 143-44.

20 Mansfield, *The challenge of a better ABC*, 13.

21 Jonathon Hutchinson, 'Extending the ABC's public service remit through ABC Pool,' *RIPE* 5-6, September (2012).; Georgie McClean, 'Maintaining relevance: Cultural diversity and the case for public service broadcasting' (paper presented at the Record of the Communications Policy & Research Forum 2008, 2008).

22 Harold Hotelling, 'Stability in Competition,' *The Economic Journal* 39, no. 153 (1929).

23 Peter O Steiner, 'Program patterns and preferences, and the workability of competition in radio broadcasting,' *The Quarterly Journal of Economics* 66, no. 2 (1952); 'Monopoly and competition in television: some policy issues,' *Manchester School of Economic and Social Studies* 29, no. 2 (1961); Gordon Hughes and David Vines, *Deregulation and the future of commercial television*, Hume paper (Aberdeen: Aberdeen University Press, 1989).

24 Glenn Withers, 'Broadcasting,' in *A handbook of cultural economics*, ed. Ruth Towse (Cheltenham, Glos, UK ; Northampton, MA: Edward Elgar, 2003).

25 Cited in B Cole, 'What's Really Preventing the Expansion of Broadcasting Services?,' *The Australian Quarterly* 38, no. 3 (1966).

26 Peter A Wells, David S Waller, and Roman Lanis, 'TV Licences in Australia: Barriers to competition, big bucks, and the impact of new media,' *Australian Journal of Communication* 39, no. 2 (2012).

27 Australian Broadcasting Tribunal, *Cable and subscription television services for Australia : report of the Inquiry by the*

Australian Broadcasting Tribunal into Cable and Subscription Television Services and Related Matters (Canberra: Australian Government Publishing Service, 1982).

28 Franco Papandrea, *Broadcasting Planning and Entrenched Protection of Incumbent Broadcasters*, 2000/1, IPA Policy Paper (Communication and Media Policy Institute; Institute of Public Affairs, 2000).

29 Gillian Doyle, *Understanding media economics* (London; Thousand Oaks, California: Sage, 2002), 75.

30 'ABC Friends predicts Rupert Murdoch's 'plans' for the ABC,' *B&T Magazine*, 23 June 2016.

31 CPD, House of Representatives, 10 March 1932, p. 957.

32 CPD, House of Representatives, 17 March 1932, p. 1256.

33 Thomas, *Broadcast and be damned: the ABC's first two decades*; Potter, *Broadcasting empire the BBC and the British world, 1922-1970.*

34 Murray Goot, 'Radio LANG,' in *Jack Lang*, ed. Heather Radi and Peter Spearritt (Neutral Bay, New South Wales: Hale & Iremonger, 1977).

35 CPD, House of Representatives, 10 March 1932, p. 957.

36 Joint Committee on Wireless Broadcasting, *Report*

37 Colm Kiernan, 'Arthur A. Calwell's clashes with the Australian Press, 1943-1945,' *University of Wollongong Historical Journal* 2, no. 1 (1976): 77.

38 Curthoys, 'Television before television.'

39 'Television service in two years', *The Canberra Times*, 15 June 1949, p. 4.

40 Inglis, *This is the ABC : the Australian Broadcasting Commission, 1932-1983*; *Whose ABC?: the Australian Broadcasting Corporation 1983-2006.*

41 Commonwealth Parliamentary Debates, Senate Environment and Communications Legislation Committee, Estimates, 5 May 2016, p. 116-140.

42 Chris Berg, *The growth of Australia's regulatory state: ideology, accountability and the mega-regulators* (Melbourne: Institute of Public Affairs, 2008).
43 Michael Warby, *Whose ABC? The ABC, staff capture and the obstacles to accountability*, vol. 11, Backgrounder (Institute of Public Affairs, 1999).
44 Cited in Potter, *Broadcasting empire the BBC and the British world, 1922-1970*, 25.
45 Alan Sunderland, 'Objective reporting: it has never been more necessary,' *ABC The Drum*, 10 September 2015.
46 See, for instance, Martin Flanagan, 'Rupert Murdoch's attack on 'our ABC' like a mediaeval siege,' *The Sydney Morning Herald*, 8 February 2014.
47 W. T. Stead, 'Government by Journalism,' *The Contemporary Review* 49, May (1886).
48 James Curran and Jean Seaton, *Power without responsibility: the press and broadcasting in Britain*, 7th ed. (London: Routledge, 2010).
49 E.M. Noam, *Media Ownership and Concentration in America* (Oxford University Press, 2009).
50 Benjamin M. Compaine and Douglas Gomery, *Who Owns the Media?: Competition and Concentration in the Mass Media Industry* (Taylor & Francis, 2000).
51 Benjamin M. Compaine, *The Media Monopoly Myth: how new competition is expanding our sources of information and entertainment* (New Millennium Research Council, 2005).
52 *Ibid.*
53 Adam D. Thierer, *Media Myths: Making sense of the debate over media ownership* (Washington D.C.: The Progress & Freedom Foundation, 2005).
54 John D. H. Downing, 'Media Ownership, Concentration, and Control: The evolution of debate,' in *The Handbook*

of Political Economy of Communications, ed. Janet Wasko, Graham Murdock, and Helena Sousa (Malden, Massachusetts: Blackwell Publishing, 2011), 155-56.

55 Compaine, T*he Media Monopoly Myth: how new competition is expanding our sources of information and entertainment*

56 Australian Broadcasting Corporation, *The ABC in the Digital Age—Towards 2020* (Australian Broadcasting Corporation, 2008).

57 We speak, of course, from experience.

58 Ludwig Von Mises, *Human Action: A Treatise on Economics* (Fox & Wilkes, 1963), 229.

59 Jerome Rothenberg, 'Consumer sovereignty and the economics of TV programming,' *Studies in Public Communication* 4, no. 1 (1962); Allan Brown, 'Economics and Diversity of Broadcasting Programmes,' *Economic Analysis and Policy* 18, no. 1 (1988).

60 CPD, House of Representatives, 17 March 1935, p. 968.

61 CPD, House of Representatives, 10 March 1935, p. 970.

62 CPD, House of Representatives, 28 April 1935, p. 83.

63 CPD, House of Representatives, 28 April 1932, p. 89.

64 Lesley Johnson, ''Sing'em Muck Clara': Highbrow versus Lowbrow on Early Australian Radio,' *Meanjin* 41, no. 2 (1982).

65 CPD, House of Representatives, 10 March 1932, p. 956.

66 Tyler Cowen, *In Praise of Commercial Culture* (Harvard University Press, 2009).

67 *Ibid.*, 182.

68 John Docker, 'Popular culture versus the state: an argument against Australian content regulations for television,' *Media Information Australia* 59, February (1991).

69 John Kleinig, *Paternalism* (Manchester University Press, 1983).

70 For libertarian paternalism see Richard H. Thaler, *Misbehaving: the making of behavioral economics* (New York: W.W. Norton & Company, 2015); Richard H. Thaler and Cass R. Sunstein, *Nudge: improving decisions about health, wealth, and happiness* (New Haven: Yale University Press, 2008). We offer a critique of libertarian paternalism in Chris Berg and Sinclair Davidson, 'Nudging, Calculation and Utopia,' *Journal of Behavioral Economics for Policy* 1, Special Issue (2017).
71 Reith, *Broadcast over Britain*, p. 2.
72 Ibid., 3.
73 Ibid., 32-34.
74 Ibid., 53.
75 Ibid., 34.
76 CPD, House of Representatives, 10 March 1932, p. 958.
77 CPD, House of Representatives, 10 March 1932, p. 959.
78 CPD, House of Representatives, 10 March 1932, p. 972.
79 Curthoys, 'Television before television,' p. 160.
80 Royal Commission on Television, *Report*
81 James Spigelman, 'Contemporary Challenges of the ABC,' Address to the National Press Club, 11 December 2013.
82 C.R. Sunstein, *Republic.com 2.0* (Princeton University Press, 2009).
83 Andrew M. Guess, 'Media Choice and Moderation: Evidence from Online Tracking Data,' (2016); Pablo Barberá, 'How social media reduces mass political polarization. Evidence from Germany, Spain, and the US,' New York University (2014); Seth Flaxman, Sharad Goel, and Justin Rao, 'Filter bubbles, echo chambers, and online news consumption,' *Public Opinion Quarterly* 80, Special issue (2016).
84 CPD, House of Representatives, 9 March 1932, p. 842.

85 Mansfield, *The challenge of a better ABC,* p. 23.
86 Australian Broadcasting Corporation, *Annual Report*
87 *Submission to the Senate Environment and Communications Legislation Committee Inquiry into the Australian Broadcasting Corporation Amendment (Rural and Regional Advocacy) Bill 2015* (2016), p. 1.
88 Mansfield, *The challenge of a better ABC,* p. 24.
89 Australian Broadcasting Corporation Amendment (Rural and Regional Advocacy) Bill 2015
90 Australian Broadcasting Corporation, *Submission to the Senate Environment and Communications Legislation Committee Inquiry into the Australian Broadcasting Corporation Amendment (Rural and Regional Advocacy) Bill 2015*
91 Media Entertainment & Arts Alliance, *Senate Standing Committees on Environment and Communications, Information Technology and the Arts Inquiry into the ABC on the matter of regional diversity* (2013).
92 Mark Scott, 'Our ABC, Our Future. A Message from Mark Scott' (2014); Media Entertainment & Arts Alliance, *Senate Standing Committees on Environment and Communications, Information Technology and the Arts Inquiry into the ABC on the matter of regional diversity*
93 Australian Bureau of Statistics, Australian Historical Population Statistics, 2014 (2014).
94 John Freebairn, 'Economic policy for rural and regional Australia,' *Australian Journal of Agricultural and Resource Economics* 47, no. 3 (2003): 412.
95 Paul Collits, 'Is there a regional Australia, and is it worth spending big on?,' *Policy: A Journal of Public Policy and Ideas* 28, no. 2 (2012).
96 *Ibid.*, 25.
97 Australian Government, *Creative Australia: National Cultural Policy* (2013).

98 Tyler Cowen, *Good and Plenty: The Creative Successes of American Arts Funding* (Princeton University Press, 2009).
99 For an alternative model of the purposes of intellectual property see Sinclair Davidson and Jason Potts, 'The Stationary Bandit Model of Intellectual Property,' *Cato Journal* 37, no. 1 (2016).
100 Screen Australia, *Convergence 2011: Australian content state of play* (Australian government, 2011).
101 Nic Christensen, 'Cheap imports killing expensive local TV productions,' *The Australian*, 25 August 2011.
102 Docker, 'Popular culture versus the state: an argument against Australian content regulations for television.'
103 On tastes and preferences, see Chris Berg, 'An Institutional Theory of Free Speech,' SSRN (2017). On the appropriate limits of government manipulation of its citizens, see *Liberty, Equality & Democracy* (Victoria: Connor Court Publishing, 2015).
104 Thomas Jefferson, 'Thomas Jefferson to the Marquis de Lafayette,' Founders Online: National Archives, 4 November 1823.
105 Robert A. Dahl, *On Democracy* (Yale University Press, 2015); C Edwin Baker, 'The media that citizens need,' *University of Pennsylvania Law Review* (1998); Alexander Meiklejohn, Political freedom: the constitutional powers of the people (Harper, 1960); 'The First Amendment is an absolute,' *The Supreme Court Review* 1961 (1961); A.M. Bickel, *The Morality of Consent* (Yale University Press, 1975).
106 William G Buss, 'Alexander Meiklejohn, American Constitutional Law, and Australia's Implied Freedom of Political Communication,' *Federal Law Review* 34 (2006).
107 Djankov et al., 'Who owns the media?.'

108 Mark Scott, 'One Sure Bet: The Future of Public Broadcasting' Address to the National Press Club, 24 February 2016.
109 CPD, House of Representatives, 24 November 1948, p. 3436.
110 CPD, House of Representatives, 10 March 1932, p. 955.
111 Curthoys, 'Television before television.'
112 CPD, House of Representatives, 28 April 1932, p. 105.

The burden of the ABC

1 William A. Niskanen, *Bureaucracy: Servant or master? Lessons from America,* Hobart Paper (London: Institute of Economic Affairs, 1973).
2 *Ibid.*, 3-4.
3 Gordon Tullock, 'Bureaucracy,' in *Government failure: A primer in public choice,* ed. Gordon Tullock, Arthur Seldon, and Gordon L. Brady (Washington D.C.: Cato Institute, 2002).
4 Inglis, *Whose ABC?: the Australian Broadcasting Corporation 1983-2006*, 160.
5 Brian McNair and Adam Swift, 'Does the ABC deliver Australians good bang for their buck?,' *The Conversation*, 30 April 2014.
6 Rhonda Jolly, *The ABC: an overview (updated)*, Parliamentary Research Paper (Commonwealth Parliamentary Library, 2014).
7 RBA inflation calculator.
8 See Armen A Alchian, 'The basis of some recent advances in the theory of management of the firm,' *The Journal of Industrial Economics* (1965); 'Corporate management and property rights,' in *Economic Policy and the Regulation of Corporate Securities,* ed. Henry Manne (Washington D.C.: American Enterprise Institute, 1969).

9 William Baumol, *Business behaviour, value and growth* (New York: MacMillan, 1959); Robin Marris, 'A model of the 'managerial' enterprise,' *The Quarterly Journal of Economics* 77, no. 2 (1963); Oliver E Williamson, 'Managerial discretion and business behavior,' *The American Economic Review* 53, no. 5 (1963).
10 CPD, Senate Select Committee on the Future of Public Interest Journalism, 17 May 2017, p. 20-21
11 Axel Bruns, 'The ABC is not siphoning audiences from Fairfax,' *The Conversation*, 26 May 2017.
12 Nick Tabakoff, 'Change ABC charter so kids get the real story,' *The Australian*, 5 June 2017.
13 One of us has been somewhat critical of these fact checking services: see Chris Berg, 'The Art Of Telling The Truth,' *ABC The Drum*, 13 November 2012.
14 Andrew Bolt, 'ABC can't keep its big advantage over private media,' *The Daily Telegraph*, 20 November 2013.
15 Sarah Martin, 'On air and off, the ABC spares no expense on its stars,' *The Australian*, 20 November 2013.
16 Jon Faine, 'ABC salary leak: Mark Scott talks to Jon Faine,' ABC Radio Melbourne, 20 November 2013.
17 Richard Posner, *Public Intellectuals: A study of decline* (Harvard University Press, 2003), p. 25.
18 Joseph A. Schumpeter, *Capitalism, socialism, and democracy* (New York, London,: Harper & Brothers, 1942), p. 147.
19 Friedrich Hayek, 'The intellectuals and socialism,' in *Studies in philosophy, politics and economics*, ed. Friedrich Hayek (Routledge, 1967).
20 Gerard Henderson, 'Devil in the detail, but it's now their job,' *The Sydney Morning Herald*, 8 March 2005.
21 Folker Hanusch, 2013, 'Journalists in times of change: evidence from a new survey of Australia's journalistic workforce', *Australian Journalism Review*, 35(1) 29-41.

22 Richard Swedberg, in Schumpeter, *Capitalism, Socialism, and Democracy,* p. xvii.
23 Chris Uhlmann, 'Plotting a balanced course in a climate of angry grievance,' *ABC The Drum,* 25 March 2011.
24 Maxwell E. McCombs and Donald L. Shaw, 'The Agenda-setting Function of Mass Media,' Public Opinion Quarterly 26, no. 2 (1972).
25 Dietram A. Scheufele, 'Framing as a theory of media effects,' *Journal of Communication*, Winter (1999).
26 Edward S. Herman and Naom Chomsky, *Manufacturing consent: The political economy of the mass media* (New York: Pantheon, 1988).
27 Ellie Large, 'STOP IPA 'Operatives' from being on ABC MEDIA whilst they push for PRIVATISING AUNTY', Change.org, https://www.change.org/p/senator-fifield-prevent-institute-of-public-affairs-operatives-from-appearing-on-all-forms-of-abc-media
28 Tim Groseclose and Jeffrey Milyo, 'A Measure of Media Bias,' *The Quarterly Journal of Economics* 120, no. 4 (2005).
29 Oliver Latham, *Bias At The BEEB?: A Quantitative Study Of Slant In BBC Online Reporting* (Centre for Policy Studies, 2014).
30 Joshua S Gans and Andrew Leigh, 'How Partisan is the Press? Multiple Measures of Media Slant,' *The Economic Record* 88, no. 280 (2012).
31 A far more robust technique would have been to identify a group of individuals at the beginning of their sample period and establish how many times they were quoted and then to have updated that list each year.
32 Margaret Simons, 'Are you thinking what I'm thinking?: How the ABC's diverse curiosity might conquer partisanship and bring us all together,' *Meanjin* 76, no. 2 (2017).
33 *Ibid.*, 62.

34 Morris Newman, 'Maurice Newman's address to ABC staff,' *The Australian*, 11 March 2010.
35 'Thoughts of the chairman,' *Sydney Morning Herald*, 12 March 2010.
36 'ABC clique in control of climate,' *The Australian*, 18 December 2012.
37 Sinclair Davidson, 'Climategate: A failure of governance,' in *Climate Change: The Facts*, ed. Alan Moran (Melbourne: Institute of Public Affairs, 2009).
38 'Aunty's Robyn Williams explains how climate deniers are as outrageous as kiddie fiddlers,' *The Australian*, 26 November 2012.
39 James Paterson, *Public broadcaster or green activist?: How the ABC spins Australia's energy choices* (Institute of Public Affairs, 2014).
40 We detail some of the political context behind this in Berg and Davidson, 'Media Regulation: A Critique of Finkelstein and Tiffen.'
41 Jessica Wright, 'ABC dumps Milne from Insiders,' *The Sydney Morning Herald*, 4 September 2011.
42 Paul Barry, 'Truth, trust and treachery,' *Media Watch*, 3 February 2014.
43 Denise Musto, Undated correspondance, *Media Watch* 2014.
44 Aaron Patrick, 'Emma Alberici anti-tax cut article contained nine errors,' *Australian Financial Review*, 10 April 2018.
45 'Is there a place in Rudd era for conservative columnists?,' *The Australian*, 8 February 2008.

The case for privatisation

1 Simons, 'Are you thinking what I'm thinking?: How the ABC's diverse curiosity might conquer partisanship and bring us all together.'
2 CPD, House of Representatives, 28 April 1932, p. 83.
3 Michael C Jensen, 'The modern industrial revolution, exit, and the failure of internal control systems,' *The Journal of Finance* 48, no. 3 (1993).
4 Peter Van Onselen, 'A billion good reasons to sell the broadcaster,' *The Australian* 2013.
5 Tony Walker, 'Why the ABC has a case to answer,' *The Weekend Financial Review,* 1 February 2014.
6 Dennis Shanahan, 'Aunty's tactical mistakes haunt it with a vengeance,' *The Weekend Australian,* 1 February 2014.
7 Bob Walker and Betty Walker, *Privatisation: sell off or sell out?: The Australian experience,* ABC Books (Sydney, New South Wales 2000).
8 'Privatisation: sell off or sell out?,' *7:30 Report,* 8 June 2000.
9 'The National Economic Debate,' *Q&A,* 19 August 2013.
10 Joe Hockey, 'Institute of Public Affairs Q&A' 31 March 2015.
11 Chris Berg, 'The socialist calculation debate,' *ABC The Drum*, 28 December 2011.
12 David E. M. Sappington and Joseph E Stiglitz, 'Privatization, Information and Incentives,' *Journal of Policy Analysis and Management* 6, no. 4 (1987).
13 William L. Megginson, *The Financial Economics of Privatization* (Oxford University Press, 2005).
14 Rajnish Mehra and Edward C Prescott, 'The equity premium: A puzzle,' *Journal of monetary Economics* 15, no. 2 (1985).

15 Simon Grant and John Quiggin, 'Public investment and the risk premium for equity,' *Economica* 70, no. 277 (2003).
16 Megginson, *The Financial Economics of Privatization*, 152.
17 Rebecca Weisser, 'Subsidy fine but balance required,' *The Australian*, 25 May 2013.
18 Megginson, *The Financial Economics of Privatization*, 388.
19 James Paterson, 'Public interest journalism: let the public pick their own winners,' *Australian Financial Review*, 18 July 2017. For some potential pitfalls of this approach, see Chris Berg, *Submission to the Senate Select Committee on the Future of Public Interest Journalism* (2017).
20 Bryan Caplan, *The Myth of the Rational Voter: Why Democracies Choose Bad Policies* (Princeton University Press, 2011).
21 See 'Commonwealth to sell C.O.R. shares at big profit,' *The Canberra Times*, 25 September 1952; 'Govt. interest in C.O.R. sold for £2,762,506,' *The Townsville Daily Bulletin*, 27 September 1952.
22 Thomas Sowell, *A Conflict of Visions: Ideological Origins of Political Struggles* (Basic Books, 2007).

Conclusion

1 On its sale, the government kept the overseas telecommunications arm in public hands. Given, 'A 50/50 proposition: public-private partnerships in Australian communications,' 107.
2 'Government to sell AWA shares at 45/-,' *Examiner*, 28 July 1951.
3 Allen and Berg, 'Subjective Political Economy.'

References

'ABC Friends predicts Rupert Murdoch's 'plans' for the ABC.' *B&T Magazine*, 23 June 2016. Available at http://www.bandt.com.au/media/abc-friends-predicts-rupert-mordochs-plans-abc.

Albon, Robert, and Franco Papandrea. *Media regulation in Australia and the public interest*. Current issues. Melbourne: Institute of Public Affairs, 1998.

Alchian, Armen A. 'The basis of some recent advances in the theory of management of the firm.' *The Journal of Industrial Economics* (1965): 30-41.

———. 'Corporate management and property rights.' In *Economic Policy and the Regulation of Corporate Securities*, edited by Henry Manne. Washington D.C.:

'ABC Friends predicts Rupert Murdoch's 'plans' for the ABC.' *B&T Magazine*, 23 June 2016. Available at http://www.bandt.com.au/media/abc-friends-predicts-rupert-mordochs-plans-abc.

Albon, Robert, and Franco Papandrea. *Media regulation in Australia and the public interest*. Current issues. Melbourne: Institute of Public Affairs, 1998.

Alchian, Armen A. 'The basis of some recent advances in the theory of management of the firm.' *The Journal of Industrial Economics* (1965): 30-41.

———. 'Corporate management and property rights.' In *Economic Policy and the Regulation of Corporate Securities*, edited by Henry Manne. Washington D.C.: American Enterprise Institute, 1969.

Allen, Darcy W.E. 'The Subjective Political Economy of Innovation Policy.' (2016).

Allen, Darcy W.E, and Chris Berg. 'Subjective Political Economy.' *New Perspectives on Political Economy* 13 no. 1-2: 19-40.

Allsop, Richard. 'How government holds back technological change.' *IPA Review* (2014).

'Aunty's Robyn Williams explains how climate deniers are as outrageous as kiddie fiddlers.' *The Australian*, 26 November 2012.

Australian Broadcasting Corporation. *The ABC in the Digital Age—Towards 2020*. Australian Broadcasting Corporation, 2008.

———. *Annual Report*. 2016.

———. *Submission to the House of Representatives Standing Committee on Communications and the Arts Inquiry into the importance of public and commercial broadcasting, online content and live production to rural and regional Australia, including the arts, news and other services*. Sydney: Australian Broadcasting Corporation, 2016.

———. *Submission to the Senate Environment and Communications Legislation Committee Inquiry into the Australian Broadcasting Corporation Amendment (Rural and Regional Advocacy) Bill 2015*. 2016.

Australian Broadcasting Tribunal. *Cable and subscription television services for Australia : report of the Inquiry by the Australian Broadcasting Tribunal into Cable and Subscription Television Services and Related Matters, August 1982*. Edited by David Jones. Canberra: Australian Government Publishing Service, 1982.

Australian Bureau of Statistics. *Australian Historical Population Statistics*. 2014.

Australian Government. *Creative Australia: National Cultural Policy*. 2013.

Bailey, Michael. 'Rethinking public service broadcasting: the historical limits to publicness.' In *Media and public spheres*, 96-108: Springer, 2007.

Baker, C. Edwin. 'The media that citizens need.' *University of Pennsylvania Law Review* (1998): 317-408.

Baker, C. Edwin. *Media, markets, and democracy*. Cambridge: Cambridge University Press, 2002.

Barberá, Pablo. 'How social media reduces mass political polarization. Evidence from Germany, Spain, and the US.' Working Paper, New York University, 2014.

Barry, Paul. 'Truth, trust and treachery.' *Media Watch*, 3 February 2014. Available at http://www.abc.net.au/mediawatch/transcripts/s3937354.htm.

Battin, Tim. 'Keynesianism, Socialism, and Labourism, and the Role of Ideas in Labor Ideology.' *Labour History*, no. 66 (1994): 33-44.

Baumol, William. *Business behaviour, value and growth*. New York: Macmillan, 1959.

Berg, Chris. 'The Art Of Telling The Truth.' *ABC The Drum*, 13 November 2012.

———. *The growth of Australia's regulatory state: ideology, accountability and the mega-regulators*. Melbourne: Institute of Public Affairs, 2008.

———. *In defence of freedom of speech: from Ancient Greece to Andrew Bolt*. Monographs on Western civilisation. Melbourne; Subiaco: Institute of Public Affairs; Mannkal Economic Education Foundation, 2012.

———. 'An Institutional Theory of Free Speech.' *SSRN* (2017).

———. *Liberty, Equality & Democracy*. Victoria: Connor Court Publishing, 2015.

———. 'Safety and soundness: an economic history of prudential bank regulation in Australia, 1893-2008.' RMIT University, 2016.

———. 'The socialist calculation debate.' *ABC The Drum*, 28 December 2011.

———. *Submission to the Senate Select Committee on the Future of Public Interest Journalism*. 2017.

Berg, Chris, and Sinclair Davidson. 'Media Regulation: A Critique of Finkelstein and Tiffen.' (2015).

———. 'Nudging, Calculation and Utopia.' *Journal of Behavioral Economics for Policy* 1, no. Special Issue (2017): 49-52.

———. 'Section 18C, Human Rights, and Media Reform: An Institutional Analysis of the 2011-13 Australian Free Speech Debate.' *Agenda: a Journal of Policy Analysis and Reform* 23, no. 1 (2016): 5.

Bickel, A.M. *The Morality of Consent*. Yale University Press, 1975.

Bolt, Andrew. 'ABC can't keep its big advantage over private media.' *The Daily Telegraph*, 20 November 2013.

Brennan, David J. 'Printing in England and Broadcasting in Australia: A Comparative Study of Regulatory Impulse.' *Adelaide Law Review* 22 (2000): 63.

Briggs, Asa. *The history of broadcasting in the United Kingdom*. London: Oxford University Press, 1961.

Brown, Allan. 'Australian public broadcasting under review: the Mansfield report on the ABC.' *Canadian Journal of Communication* 26, no. 1 (2001): 107.

———. 'Economics and Diversity of Broadcasting Programmes.' *Economic Analysis and Policy* 18, no. 1 (1988): 43-52.

Bruns, Axel. 'The ABC is not siphoning audiences from Fairfax.' *The Conversation*, 26 May 2017.

Burns, R. W. *British television: the formative years*. London: P. Peregrinus, 1986.

———. *Television: an international history of the formative years*. London: Institution of Engineering and Technology, 1998.

Buss, William G. 'Alexander Meiklejohn, American Constitutional Law, and Australia's Implied Freedom of Political Communication.' *Federal Law Review* 34 (2006): 421.

Caplan, Bryan. *The Myth of the Rational Voter: Why Democracies Choose Bad Policies*. Princeton University Press, 2011.

Christensen, Nic. 'Cheap imports killing expensive local TV productions.' *The Australian*, 25 August 2011.

Cole, B. 'What's Really Preventing the Expansion of Broadcasting Services?'. *The Australian Quarterly* 38, no. 3 (1966): 72-87.

Collits, Paul. 'Is there a regional Australia, and is it worth spending big on?'. *Policy: A Journal of Public Policy and Ideas* 28, no. 2 (2012): 24.

Committee of Review of the Australian Broadcasting Commission. *ABC in Review: National Broadcasting in the 1980s.* Canberra: Australian Government Publishing Service, 1981.

'Commonwealth to sell C.O.R. shares at big profit.' *The Canberra Times*, 25 September 1952.

Compaine, Benjamin M. *The Media Monopoly Myth: how new competition is expanding our sources of information and entertainment.* New Millennium Research Council, 2005.

Compaine, Benjamin M., and Douglas Gomery. *Who Owns the Media?: Competition and Concentration in the Mass Media Industry.* Taylor & Francis, 2000.

Cowen, Tyler. *Good and Plenty: The Creative Successes of American Arts Funding.* Princeton University Press, 2009.

———. *In Praise of Commercial Culture.* Harvard University Press, 2009.

Coyne, Christopher J., and Peter T. Leeson. *Media, development and institutional change.* New thinking in political economy. Cheltenham: E. Elgar, 2009.

Curnow, Ross. 'The origins of Australian broadcasting, 1900–23.' In *Initiative and Organisation*, edited by Ian Bedford and Ross Curnow. Melbourne: F.W. Cheshire, 1963.

Curran, James, and Jean Seaton. *Power without responsibility: the press and broadcasting in Britain.* 7th ed. London: Routledge, 2010.

Curthoys, Ann. 'Television before television.' *Continuum: Journal of Media & Cultural Studies* 4, no. 2 (1991): 152-70.

Dahl, Robert A. *On Democracy.* Yale University Press, 1998.

Davidson, Sinclair. 'The ABC Charter is not 'Law'', *Catallaxy Files*, 11 October 2016. Available at http://catallaxy-files.com/2016/10/11/the-abc-charter-is-not-law/.

———. 'Climategate: A failure of governance.' In *Climate Change: The Facts*, edited by Alan Moran. Melbourne: Institute of Public Affairs, 2009.

———. 'Environmental protest: an economics of regulation approach.' *Australian Environment Review* 29, no. 10 (2014): 283-86.

———. *Productivity enhancing regulatory reform*. Australia Adjusting: Optimising national prosperity. 2013.

———. 'Why have an ABC at all?' *ABC The Drum*, 20 December 2011.

Davidson, Sinclair, and Jason Potts. 'A new institutional approach to innovation policy.' *Australian Economic Review* 49, no. 2 (2016): 200-07.

———. 'Social costs and the institutions of innovation policy.' (2015).

———. 'The Stationary Bandit Model of Intellectual Property.' *Cato Journal* 37, no. 1 (2016): 69-88.

Davis, Glyn. *Breaking up the ABC*. Sydney: Allen & Unwin, 1988.

Day, Mark. 'Scott's talk of ABC being a market failure is cheap.' *The Australian*, 23 May 2011.

Deloitte. *Media Consumer Survey 2016: Australian media and digital preferences*. 2016.

———. *Media Consumer Survey 2016: The Australian Cut, Hyper connectivity: Clever consumption*. 2016.

Department of Communications. *ABC and SBS Efficiency Study: Draft Report*. 2014.

Department of Transport and Communications. *Review of national broadcasting policy*. Canberra: Australian Government Publishing Service, 1988.

Dixon, Michael Francis. *Inside the ABC: a piece of Australian history*. Melbourne: Hawthorn Press, 1975.

Djankov, Simeon, Edward Glaeser, Rafael La Porta, Florencio Lopez-de-Silanes, and Andrei Shleifer. 'The new comparative economics.' *Journal of comparative economics* 31, no. 4 (2003): 595-619.

Djankov, Simeon, Caralee McLiesh, Tatiana Nenova, and Andrei Shleifer. 'Who owns the media?'. *Journal of Law and Economics* 46 (2003).

Docker, John. 'Popular culture versus the state: an argument against Australian content regulations for television.' *Media Information Australia* 59, February (1991): 7-26.

Dörr, Jonathan, Thomas Wagner, Alexander Benlian, and Thomas Hess. 'Music as a Service as an Alternative to Music Piracy?'. *Business & Information Systems Engineering* 5, no. 6 (2013): 383-96.

Douglas, Susan J. *Inventing American broadcasting, 1899-1922.* Baltimore: Johns Hopkins University Press, 1987.

Downing, John D. H. 'Media Ownership, Concentration, and Control: The evolution of debate.' In *The Handbook of Political Economy of Communications*, edited by Janet Wasko, Graham Murdock and Helena Sousa, 140-68. Malden, Massachusetts: Blackwell Publishing, 2011.

Doyle, Gillian. *Understanding media economics.* London; Thousand Oaks, California: Sage, 2002.

Epstein, David, and Sharyn O'Halloran. 'Administrative procedures, information, and agency discretion.' *American Journal of Political Science* (1994): 697-722.

Faine, Jon. 'ABC salary leak: Mark Scott talks to Jon Faine.' *ABC Radio Melbourne*, 20 November 2013. Available at http://www.abc.net.au/local/audio/2013/11/20/3895003.htm.

Faine, Jon, and Bruce Guthrie. 'Is there a place in Rudd era for conservative columnists?'. *The Australian*, 8 February 2008.

Fessenden, H. May Trott. *Fessenden, builder of tomorrows*. New York: Coward-McCann, 1940.

Fitzgerald, Julian. *On message: political communications of Australian prime ministers 1901-2014*. Mawson: Clareville Press, 2014.

Flanagan, Martin. 'Rupert Murdoch's attack on 'our ABC' like a mediaeval siege.' *Sydney Morning Herald*, 8 February 2014.

Flaxman, Seth, Sharad Goel, and Justin Rao. 'Filter bubbles, echo chambers, and online news consumption.' *Public Opinion Quarterly* 80, Special issue (2016): 298-320.

Freebairn, John. 'Economic policy for rural and regional Australia.' *Australian Journal of Agricultural and Resource Economics* 47, no. 3 (2003): 389-414.

Friedewald, Michael. 'Telefunken vs. Marconi, or the Race for Wireless Telegraphy at Sea, 1896-1914.' *SSRN* (2012).

Gans, Joshua S, and Andrew Leigh. 'How Partisan is the Press? Multiple Measures of Media Slant.' *The Economic Record* 88, no. 280 (2012): 127-47.

Given, Jock. 'A 50/50 proposition: public-private partnerships in Australian communications.' *Media International Australia* 129, no. 1 (2008): 104-15.

Goot, Murray. 'Radio LANG.' In *Jack Lang*, edited by Heather Radi and Peter Spearritt, 119-37. Neutral Bay, New South Wales: Hale & Iremonger, 1977.

'Government to sell AWA shares at 45/-.' *Examiner*, 28 July 1951.

'Govt. interest in C.O.R. sold for £2,762,506.' *Townsville Daily Bulletin*, 27 September 1952.

Grant, Simon, and John Quiggin. 'Public investment and the risk premium for equity.' *Economica* 70, no. 277 (2003): 1-18.

Green, F. J. *Australian broadcasting: a report on the structure of the Australian broadcasting system and associated matters*. Canberra: Postal and Telecommunications Department, 1977.

Griffen-Foley, Bridget. 'The birth of a hybrid: the shaping of the Australian radio industry.' *Radio Journal: International Studies in Broadcast & Audio Media* 2, no. 3 (2004): 153-69.

———. *Changing stations: the story of Australian commercial radio*. Sydney: UNSW Press, 2009.

Groseclose, Tim, and Jeffrey Milyo. 'A Measure of Media Bias.' *The Quarterly Journal of Economics* 120, no. 4 (2005): 1191-237.

Guess, Andrew M. 'Media Choice and Moderation: Evidence from Online Tracking Data.' 2016.

Hayek, Friedrich. 'The intellectuals and socialism.' In *Studies in philosophy, politics and economics*, edited by Friedrich Hayek: Routledge, 1967.

———. 'The use of knowledge in society.' *The American Economic Review* (1945): 519-30.

Hazlett, Thomas W. *The Political Spectrum: the tumultuous liberation of wireless technology, from Herbert Hoover to the smartphone*. New Haven and London: Yale University Press, 2017.

Henderson, Gerard. 'Devil in the detail, but it's now their job.' *Sydney Morning Herald*, 8 March 2005.

Herman, Edward S., and Noam Chomsky. *Manufacturing consent: The political economy of the mass media*. New York: Pantheon, 1988.

Hockey, Joe. 'Institute of Public Affairs Q&A' 31 March 2015. Available at http://jbh.ministers.treasury.gov.au/transcript/069-2015/.

Home, R. W. 'Threlfall, Sir Richard (1861-1932).' Carlton,

Victoria: Melbourne University Publishing, 1990.
Hong, Sungook. *Wireless: from Marconi's black-box to the audion*. Cambridge: MIT Press, 2001.
Hotelling, Harold. 'Stability in Competition.' *The Economic Journal* 39, no. 153 (1929): 41-57.
Hughes, Gordon, and David Vines. *Deregulation and the future of commercial television*. Hume paper. Aberdeen: Aberdeen University Press, 1989.
Hutchinson, Jonathon. 'Extending the ABC's public service remit through ABC Pool.' *RIPE* 5-6, September (2012).
Independent Review Panel. *The Future Funding of the BBC*. Department for Culture, Media and Sport, 1999.
Inglis, Kenneth Stanley. *This is the ABC: the Australian Broadcasting Commission, 1932-1983*. Carlton: Melbourne University Press, 1983.
———. *Whose ABC? : the Australian Broadcasting Corporation 1983-2006*. Melbourne: Black Inc., 2006.
Jefferson, Thomas. 'Thomas Jefferson to the Marquis de Lafayette.' *Founders Online*: National Archives, 4 November 1823. Available at https://founders.archives.gov/documents/Jefferson/98-01-02-3843
Jensen, Michael C. 'The modern industrial revolution, exit, and the failure of internal control systems.' *The Journal of Finance* 48, no. 3 (1993): 831-80.
Johnson, Lesley. "Sing'em Muck Clara': Highbrow versus Lowbrow on Early Australian Radio.' *Meanjin* 41, no. 2 (1982): 210.
———. *The Unseen voice : a cultural study of early Australian radio*. London: Routledge, 1988.
Joint Committee on Wireless Broadcasting. *Report*. The Parliament of the Commonwealth of Australia, 1942.
Jolly, Rhonda. *The ABC: an overview (updated)*. Parliamen-

tary Research Paper. Commonwealth Parliamentary Library, 2014.

Kiernan, Colm. 'Arthur A. Calwell's clashes with the Australian Press, 1943-1945.' *University of Wollongong Historical Journal* 2, no. 1 (1976): 74-111.

Kleinig, John. *Paternalism*. Manchester University Press, 1983.

KPMG. *Funding Adequacy and Efficiency Review*. 2006.

Langhans, Ron. *The First Twelve Months of Radio Broadcasting in Australia: 1923-1924*. Historical Radio Society of Australia, 2013.

Latham, Oliver. *Bias At The BEEB?: A Quantitative Study Of Slant In BBC Online Reporting*. Centre for Policy Studies, 2014.

Large, Ellie. 'STOP IPA 'Operatives' from being on ABC MEDIA whilst they push for PRIVATISING AUNTY', *Change.org*, https://www.change.org/p/senator-fifield-prevent-institute-of-public-affairs-operatives-from-appearing-on-all-forms-of-abc-media

Levin, Harvey Joshua. *Fact and fancy in television regulation: an economic study of policy alternatives*. New York: Russell Sage Foundation, 1980.

Mac Donald, Heather. 'Great Courses, Great Profits.' *City Journal*, Summer (2011).

MacDonald, Trent. 'Theory of unbundled and non-territorial governance: studies in evolutionary political economy.' PhD Thesis, RMIT University, 2015.

Mansfield, Bob. *The challenge of a better ABC*. Canberra: Australian Government Publishing Service, 1997.

Marris, Robin. 'A model of the 'managerial' enterprise.' *The Quarterly Journal of Economics* 77, no. 2 (1963): 185-209.

Martin, Sarah. 'On air and off, the ABC spares no expense on its stars.' *The Australian*, 20 November 2013.

McClean, Georgie. 'Maintaining relevance: Cultural diversity and the case for public service broadcasting.' Paper presented at the Record of the Communications Policy & Research Forum 2008, 2008.

McCombs, Maxwell E., and Donald L. Shaw. 'The Agenda-setting Function of Mass Media.' *Public Opinion Quarterly* 26, no. 2 (1972): 176-87.

McNair, Brian, and Adam Swift. 'Does the ABC deliver Australians good bang for their buck?' *The Conversation*, 30 April 2014.

McQuail, Denis. *Media performance: mass communication and the public interest*. London: Sage, 1992.

Media Entertainment & Arts Alliance. *Senate Standing Committees on Environment and Communications, Information Technology and the Arts Inquiry into the ABC on the matter of regional diversity*. 2013.

Megginson, William L. *The Financial Economics of Privatization*. Oxford University Press, 2005.

Mehra, Rajnish, and Edward C Prescott. 'The equity premium: A puzzle.' *Journal of Monetary Economics* 15, no. 2 (1985): 145-61.

Meiklejohn, Alexander. 'The First Amendment is an absolute.' *The Supreme Court Review* 1961 (1961): 245-66.

———. *Political freedom: the constitutional powers of the people*. Harper, 1960.

Moran, Albert. 'Some beginnings for Australian television.' *Continuum: Journal of Media & Cultural Studies* 4, no. 2 (1991): 171-83.

Moyal, Ann Mozley. *Clear across Australia: a history of telecommunications*. Melbourne, Vic: Nelson, 1984.

Musto, Denise. Undated Correspondance, *Media Watch* 2014. Available at http://www.abc.net.au/mediawatch/transcripts/1333_abcresponse.pdf

'The National Economic Debate,' Q&A, 19 August 2013. Available at http://www.abc.net.au/tv/qanda/txt/s3813523.htm.

Newman, Maurice. 'ABC clique in control of climate.' *The Australian*, 18 December 2012.

———. 'Maurice Newman's address to ABC staff.' *The Australian*, 11 March 2010.

Niskanen, William A. *Bureaucracy: Servant or master? Lessons from America*. Hobart Paper. London: Institute of Economic Affairs, 1973.

Noam, E.M. *Media Ownership and Concentration in America*. Oxford: Oxford University Press, 2009.

Owen, Bruce M. 'The economic view of programming.' *Journal of Communication* 28, no. 2 (1978): 43-47.

Papandrea, Franco. *Broadcasting Planning and Entrenched Protection of Incumbent Broadcasters*. IPA Policy Paper. 2000/1: Communication and Media Policy Institute; Institute of Public Affairs, 2000.

Paterson, James. *Public broadcaster or green activist?: How the ABC spins Australia's energy choices*. Institute of Public Affairs, 2014.

———. 'Public interest journalism: let the public pick their own winners.' *Australian Financial Review*, 18 July 2017.

Pleatsikas, Christopher, and David Teece. 'The analysis of market definition and market power in the context of rapid innovation.' *International Journal of Industrial Organization* 19, no. 5 (2001): 665-93.

Posner, Richard. *Public Intellectuals: A study of decline*. Harvard University Press, 2003.

Potter, Simon James. *Broadcasting empire: the BBC and the British world, 1922-1970*. Oxford: Oxford University Press, 2012.

'Privatisation: sell off or sell out?,' *7:30 Report*, 8 June 2000. Available at https://web.archive.org/web/20050306193836/http://www.abc.net.au/7.30/stories/s138632.htm.

Reith, J.C.W. *Broadcast over Britain*. London: Hodder and Stoughton, 1924.

———. *Memorandum of Information on the Scope and Conduct of the Broadcasting Service*. Caversham, Reading: BBC Written Archive, 1925.

Roberts, G.A. 'Business interests and the formation of the ABC.' *Politics* 7, no. 2 (1972): 149-54.

Rothenberg, Jerome. 'Consumer sovereignty and the economics of TV programming.' *Studies in Public Communication* 4, no. 1 (1962).

Royal Commission on Television. *Report*. Canberra: Commonwealth of Australia, 1954.

Royal Commission on Wireless. *Report*. The Parliament of the Commonwealth of Australia, 1927.

Sabbagh, Dan. 'ABC director general Mark Scott gives his perspective on the BBC's travails.' *Guardian*, 16 May 2011.

Sappington, David E. M., and Joseph E. Stiglitz. 'Privatization, Information and Incentives.' *Journal of Policy Analysis and Management* 6, no. 4 (1987): 567-82.

Sawer, Geoffrey. *Australian federal politics and law, 1929-1949*. Melbourne: Melbourne University Press, 1963.

Scannell, Paddy. 'Public service broadcasting: the history of a concept.' *Understanding television* (1990): 11-29.

Scheufele, Dietram A. 'Framing as a theory of media effects.' *Journal of Communication*, Winter (1999): 103-22.

Schumpeter, Joseph A. *Capitalism, socialism, and democracy*. New York, London: Harper & Brothers, 1942.

Scott, Mark. 'One Sure Bet: The Future of Public Broadcasting'. Address to the National Press Club, 24 February 2016.

———. 'Our ABC, Our Future. A Message from Mark Scott' 2014. Available at http://about.abc.net.au/our-abc-our-future/.

Screen Australia. *Convergence 2011: Australian content state of play*. Australian government, 2011.

Shanahan, Dennis. 'Aunty's tactical mistakes haunt it with a vengeance.' *Weekend Australian*, 1 February 2014.

Shepsle, Kenneth A. 'Bureaucratic drift, coalitional drift, and time consistency: A comment on Macey.' *Journal of Law, Economics, & Organization* 8, no. 1 (1992): 111-18.

Shleifer, Andrei. *The failure of judges and the rise of regulators*. Cambridge: MIT Press, 2012.

Simons, Margaret. 'Are you thinking what I'm thinking?: How the ABC's diverse curiosity might conquer partisanship and bring us all together.' *Meanjin* 76, no. 2 (2017): 44-62.

Smith, Adam. *An inquiry into the nature and causes of the wealth of nations*. Chicago: University of Chicago Press, 1976. (1776).

Sowell, Thomas. *A Conflict of Visions: Ideological Origins of Political Struggles*. Basic Books, 2007.

Spigelman, James. 'Contemporary Challenges of the ABC.' Address to the National Press Club, 11 December 2013.

Stead, W.T. 'Government by Journalism.' *The Contemporary Review* 49, May (1886): 653-74.

Steiner, Peter O. 'Monopoly and competition in television: some policy issues.' *Manchester School of Economic and Social Studies* 29, no. 2 (1961): 107-31.

———. 'Program patterns and preferences, and the workability of competition in radio broadcasting.' *The Quarterly Journal of Economics* 66, no. 2 (1952): 194-223.

Sunderland, Alan. 'Objective reporting: it has never been more necessary.' *ABC The Drum*, 10 September 2015.

Sunstein, C.R. *Republic.com 2.0*. Princeton University Press, 2009.

Tabakoff, Nick. 'Change ABC charter so kids get the real story.' *The Australian*, 5 June 2017.

Thaler, Richard H. *Misbehaving: the making of behavioral economics*. New York: W.W. Norton & Company, 2015.

Thaler, Richard H., and Cass R. Sunstein. *Nudge: improving decisions about health, wealth, and happiness*. New Haven: Yale University Press, 2008.

Thierer, Adam D. *Media Myths: Making sense of the debate over media ownership*. Washington D.C.: The Progress & Freedom Foundation, 2005.

Thomas, Alan. *Broadcast and be damned: the ABC's first two decades*. Carlton: Melbourne University Press, 1980.

'Thoughts of the chairman.' *Sydney Morning Herald*, 12 March 2010.

Tucker, Harry. 'This is how many people use Snapchat, LinkedIn, Twitter and Facebook in Australia.' *Business Insider Australia*, 31 March 2016.

Tullock, Gordon. 'Bureaucracy.' In *Government failure: A primer in public choice*, edited by Gordon Tullock, Arthur Seldon and Gordon L. Brady. Washington D.C.: Cato Institute, 2002.

Uhlmann, Chris. 'Plotting a balanced course in a climate of angry grievance.' *ABC The Drum*, 25 March 2011.

van Onselen, Peter. 'A billion good reasons to sell the broadcaster.' *The Australian*, 25 May 2013.

von Mises, Ludwig. *Human Action: A Treatise on Economics*. Fox & Wilkes, 1963.

Walker, Bob, and Betty Walker. *Privatisation: sell off or sell out?: The Australian experience*. Sydney: ABC Books, 2000.

Walker, Jesse. *Rebels on the air: an alternative history of radio in America*. New York: New York University Press, 2001.

Walker, Tony. 'Why the ABC has a case to answer.' *Weekend Financial Review*, 1 February 2014.

Warby, Michael. *Whose ABC? The ABC, staff capture and the obstacles to accountability*. Backgrounder. Vol. 11: Institute of Public Affairs, 1999.

Wasser, Frederick. *Veni, vidi, video: the Hollywood empire and the VCR*. Austin: University of Texas Press, 2001.

Weisser, Rebecca. 'Subsidy fine but balance required.' *The Australian*, 25 May 2013.

Wells, Peter A., David S. Waller, and Roman Lanis. 'TV Licences in Australia: Barriers to competition, big bucks, and the impact of new media.' *Australian Journal of Communication* 39, no. 2 (2012): 59.

White, Dominic. 'Mistake or two but still our ABC, says chair.' *Australian Financial Review*, 20 December 2014.

Williamson, Oliver E. 'Managerial discretion and business behavior.' *The American Economic Review* 53, no. 5 (1963): 1032-57.

Withers, Glenn. 'Broadcasting.' In *A handbook of cultural economics*, edited by Ruth Towse. Cheltenham, UK ; Northampton, MA: Edward Elgar, 2003.

Wright, Jessica. 'ABC dumps Milne from Insiders.' *Sydney Morning Herald*, 4 September 2011.

www.ingramcontent.com/pod-product-compliance
Lightning Source LLC
Chambersburg PA
CBHW050713280326
41926CB00088B/3013

* 9 7 8 1 9 2 5 5 0 1 8 9 6 *